MEMOIRS

OF

MADAME MALIBRAN,

BY

THE COUNTESS DE MERLIN,

AND OTHER INTIMATE FRIENDS.

WITH A

SELECTION FROM HER CORRESPONDENCE,

AND NOTICES OF THE

PROGRESS OF THE MUSICAL DRAMA

IN ENGLAND.

SECOND EDITION.

IN TWO VOLUMES.

VOL. I.

LONDON:

HENRY COLBURN, PUBLISHER,

GREAT MARLBOROUGH STREET.

1844.

PREFACE.

THE admiration created by the lamented subject of these Memoirs has been no less general than the interest excited by her untimely death. Her genius was of a most exalted character, comprehending a perception of whatever was purely intellectual in the resources of the art she had so thoroughly studied, with an intimate knowledge of the most prominent phenomena of human passion. But the characteristics of her moral nature were equally admirable with those proper to her mind. Her charity was unbounded; her sympathies so delicately sensitive, that the slightest appeal was sufficient to

bring them into most active and liberal operation; and her disposition was of that rare description which regards such kindly doings as the
manifestations of a genuine humanity.

She was eccentric, it is true, and occasionally
indulged in extravagances not perfectly feminine, which were, however, injurious to no one
but herself. These faults, if faults they must
be called, were the natural results of an imperfect education. Her father had laboured only
to make her a musician, and a musician she
became. Great natural talent there is no doubt
she possessed; but to long and severe schooling
much of its splendid results may fairly be attributed. The nobility of her character was of
her own formation. She had no lessons in
moral excellence, and her only examples of conduct were not such as could influence her with
any beneficial effect.

The biography of a being so gloriously gifted
cannot be read without profit; and to make it
as interesting as possible, it has been thought

advisable to publish in this work the observations of no less than three individuals—the most intimate of her associates—by whose united labours we are enabled to obtain the only perfect portraiture of her the public is likely to possess. There are few readers to whom the varied story of her life has not considerable attractions; but to the lover of music it must be particularly pleasing. To him, therefore, it is more particularly addressed; and with the hope that it may satisfactorily fulfil its objects, the Essays here introduced, in illustration of the progress of operatic music in this country, have been added.

CONTENTS

OF THE FIRST VOLUME.

CHAPTER I.

CHAPTER II.

CHAPTER VI.

CHAPTER VII.

CHAPTER VIII.

CHAPTER IX.

CHAPTER X.

CHAPTER XI.

CHAPTER XII.

CHAPTER XIII.

CHAPTER XIV.

CHAPTER XV.

CHAPTER XVI.

CHAPTER XVII.

CHAPTER XVIII.

CHAPTER XIX.

CHAPTER XX.

CHAPTER XXI.

CHAPTER XXII.

CHAPTER XXIII.

CHAPTER XXIV.

CHAPTER XXV.

CHAPTER XXVI.

CHAPTER XXVII.

CHAPTER XXVIII.

CHAPTER XXIX.

CHAPTER XXX.

CHAPTER XXXI.

CHAPTER XXXII.

CHAPTER XXXIII.

CHAPTER XXXVIII.

CHAPTER XXXIX.

CHAPTER XL.

CHAPTER XLI.

CHAPTER XLII.

CHAPTER XLIII.

INTRODUCTION.

PROGRESS OF THE ITALIAN OPERA IN ENGLAND
PREVIOUS TO THE PERFORMANCES OF MALIBRAN.

AT the commencement of the eighteenth century, foreign fashions began to be so generally
adopted in the higher circles of English society,
as to call forth the animadversions of the editor
of the Spectator.   In an amusing article on this
subject, Addison, confines his remarks exclu-
sively to the adoption of French customs by his
countrywomen, one of whom he describes as
receiving company in her bed-room; the last

Parisian novelty introduced by those ladies who
professed to have seen the world. " As I love
to see everything that is new," he observes, " I
once prevailed upon my friend, Will Honey-
comb, to carry me along with him to one of
these travelled ladies, desiring him at the same
time to present me as a foreigner who could not
speak English, that so I might not be obliged
to bear a part in the discourse. The lady,
though willing to appear undressed, had put on
her best looks, and painted herself for our
reception. Her hair appeared in a very *nice*
disorder, and the night-gown, which was thrown
upon her shoulders, was ruffled *with great
care.*"

Our admirable essayist has omitted in this
paper all mention of the foreign amusements
which the travelled ladies were at this period
bent upon introducing into England. Their
native theatrical entertainments, though supported by the talent of Betterton, and even the
still more popular puppet-shows, were losing all

attraction in their eyes, in consequence of their desire to indulge themselves in London in performances similar to those they had enjoyed abroad. The first steps towards the consummation of this desire appeared in various concerts and interludes, wherein foreign singers were introduced to public notice under the designations of " an Italian lady;" *Signor Gasparini, Signora Francesca, Margarita de l'Epine,* with her sister " *Maria Margherita.*" The performances of these individuals formed the principal subject of conversation at *basset* and *crimp,* at the assembly, and the club ; and their popularity led to the getting up of an opera " in the Italian manner" at one of the theatres. Thomas Clayton, a member of the royal band, produced at Drury Lane the first attempt of this kind, which was an English version of an opera performed at Venice, in the year 1677. He styled it " Arsinoe, Queen of Cyprus." It was sung in recitative, as in the original, and exhibited to the public by private subscription,

c 2

as well as by money taken at the doors of the
playhouse. It was followed by another translation, entitled " Camilla," got up in a similar
manner.

These operas succeeding, Congreve and Sir
John Vanbrugh, on the first night of opening
their new Haymarket Theatre, performed a translated opera called the " Temple of Love:" but the
music being German, and the fashion of that
time, as at the present, inclining chiefly towards
the compositions of Italian masters, the speculation of these old dramatists was not a successful
one. Addison endeavoured to administer to
the growing taste by writing an opera called
" Rosamond," to which Thomas Clayton attempted to compose; but as this was not only
not an Italian production, but about the
poorest stuff that ever assumed the name of
music, its existence lasted only three nights.
It was succeeded by " Thomyris, Queen of
Scythia," from the pen of Motteux, with a
selection from the compositions of Scarlatti and

Bononcini; which, although not so much re-
lished at first as " Camilla," the following
season rivalled it in popularity for a period of
six weeks—they being then played at Drury
Lane on alternate nights.

In these operas the performers were a motley
crew, half English and half Italian; and as it
was not always possible for the latter to employ
the translation, some were heard singing their portion of the libretto in their native tongue, while
their coadjutors proceeded in English. The
most celebrated of them were Valentini Urbani,
an Italian female styled "the Baroness," Hughes,
Lawrence, Ramondon, Leveridge, Margarita,
Mrs. Tofts, Mrs. Lindsey, and Mrs. Turner.

As an example of the *poetry* of these trans-
lations, we give the following passages from
" Love's Triumph."

> " No more trial
> Nor denial ;
> Be more kind,
> And tell your mind ;

So tost,

So crost,

I'm sad,

I'm mad ;

No more then hide your good nature,

Thou dear creature !

Balk no longer

Love nor hunger,

Both grow stronger

When they're younger ;

But pall

And fall

At last,

If long we fast."

In the following year an effort was made to introduce French dancing in a new pastoral opera called " Love's Triumph," written by Cardinal Ottoboni, the music by Carlo Cesarini Giovanni and Francesco Gasparini; but it was in vain to make any attempt to divert popular taste from Italian music. The ensuing winter was distinguished by the arrival in this country of the celebrated Nicolini Grimaldi—the Nico-

lini mentioned by Addison in his journal of a
Woman of Fashion. He appeared in a translated piece entitled " Pyrrhus and Demetrius,"
originally written by Adriano Morselli, with
music by Alessandro Scarlatti, but now arranged, with a new overture and additional
airs, by Nicolo Haym. Nicolini sang Italian ;
but despite of the confusion of the two languages exhibited in the opera in which he
performed, it speedily became so great a
favourite that he chose it for his own benefit,
which took place January 5th, 1709. This
singer was exceedingly fashionable, and obtained
eight hundred guineas for his services for the
season. At that period this was thought an
enormous sum, but it is little more than a
week's salary for some of our performers of the
present day.

The confusion of tongues occasioned by one
part of an opera being sung in Italian, and
another in English, having at last been found
intolerable, the first performed entirely in

Italian was produced in January 1710. It was
called " Almahide," and the music has been
attributed to Bononcini. Nicolini and Margarita took the principal parts, and in the
productions allotted them they were enabled to
exhibit vocal effects hitherto unknown in England. The music became remarkably popular.
The composers most approved of appear to
have been Scarlatti, Gasparini, and Bononcini,
till Handel arrived in this country, when in the
following year he produced in a fortnight his
" Rinaldo," which speedily placed him on a
footing with those distinguished masters. After
its success he was employed every season in
furnishing new productions for the operatic
company then performing at the Queen's Theatre—as the Opera House was at that time
called. There he brought out his pastoral, " Il
Pastor Fido," which lasting only four nights, was
followed in the succeeding year by his tragedy
" Teseo," which was performed twelve times.
In May 1715, the same eminent composer pro-

duced his " Amadigi: that enjoyed a more favourable reception, and in the following February was repeated by command. This season was also distinguished by the introduction of the *viol d'amour*, an instrument which was first heard in this country in a symphony performed by Signor Attilio Ariosti, between the acts of Amadigi. During this period several other operas were played, but they met with no great success, and the company was dissolved in 1717.

The Italian opera, however, had obtained too many admirers in England to be thus easily disposed of; and although for three years no performance of the kind was attempted, the leaders of the fashionable world were busily employed in endeavouring to re-establish it on a more solid foundation. With this object in view, in 1720 a fund of £50,000 was raised by subscription, to which the king contributed £1,000, to found an establishment, consisting of a governor, deputy-governor, and twenty directors, for the support and cultivation of musical genius in this country. Noblemen of the highest rank, and gentlemen of great wealth and influence, speedily became its officers. It was styled the Royal Academy of Music, and the patronage it possessed enabled the directors to engage the services of the three most eminent musicians then known, in order to create an Italian opera in England worthy of rivalling that in other countries: these were Bononcini, Attilio, and Handel. The last was started off in search of a company, and at Dresden he engaged Senesino, Berenstadt, Boschi, and the Durastanti, performers of the highest celebrity. The house opened, in April 1720, with the opera called " Numitor," composed by Giovanni Porta of Venice, with scenery and decorations superior to those of any previous operatic representation seen in this country; but it not being approved of, Handel, five nights afterwards, produced his first production for the Royal Academy of Music, " Radamisto," which, though

only in the first season sustaining ten performances, ultimately obtained considerable popularity.

The " Narcisa" of Domenico Scarlatti was
brought out May 30th, but was endured only
five nights. In the autumn all the company
had arrived, and Bononcini's " Astarto" was
represented with considerable success, but without producing any great sensation. The performances of the season, 1721, were " Radamisto"
once, " Astarto" four times, a new pasticcio
called " Arsace," and a new opera called " Mu-
zio," in three acts ; of which the first was composed by Attilio, the second by Bononcini, and
the third by Handel. The following year the
novelties were Handel's " Floridante," " Ottone,"
and " Flavius;" Bononcini's " Crispo," and
" Erminia;" and " Caius Marcius Coriolanus,"
by Attilio Ariosti. Notwithstanding, however,
the great exertions made by these celebrated composers, carried on with unabated vigour for several
years, assisted by the talents of Senesino, and

the rest of the company, the speculation was not
successful. The subscribers were dilatory in pay-
ing their subscriptions, and the public papers contained advertisements threatening the defaulters
with exposure of their names and the " utmost
rigour of the law." This method of making
patrons did not succeed, for the court of directors continued year after year to call for fresh
payments, and in 1728 it was discovered that
the whole of the £50,000 had been expended,
together with the funds resulting from the sale
of tickets, and from the sums paid for admission
at the doors, whilst debts had been incurred to
a large amount. Here ended the Royal Academy of Music, but the Italian Opera still
survived, as we find from this advertisement:
" Mr. Handel, who is just returned from Italy,
has contracted with the following persons to
perform in the Italian operas; Signor Ber-
nacchi, who is esteemed the best singer in
Italy; Signora Merighi, a woman of a very fine
presence, an excellent actress, and a very good

singer, with a counter-tenor voice; Signora
Strada, who hath a very fine treble voice, a
person of singular merit; Signor Annibale Pio
Fabri, a most excellent tenor, and a fine voice;
his wife, who performs a man's part exceeding
well; Signora Bertoldi, who has a very fine
treble voice; she is also a very genteel actress,
both in men and women's parts; a bass voice
from Hamburgh, there being none worth engag-
ing in Italy."

This company fared no better than the
preceding one. Although Handel brought out
a multitude of clever productions, and obtained
the assistance of the finest masters that were to
be found, the Italian opera in England was not
increasing in popularity. The Earl of Middle-
sex, at the head of a small body of noblemen
and gentlemen, supported him for several years,
but their assistance was not always wisely
rendered, and in the end produced more mis-
chief than good. It was not for want of liberality
that the speculation was not successful. Sene-

sino obtained fifteen hundred guineas for a single season, and Farinelli, who was more popular in England than even Nicolino, after a short sojourn here acquired a fortune, purchased an estate in his own country, and to show his gratitude to the source whence his wealth had been derived, erected there a temple, and had it dedicated to English folly. When Farinelli left the opera company in the Haymarket, it was abandoned by the directors. Heidegger became its lessee, and engaged Handel to superintend its performances; but the patronage he received was so limited, that towards the close of the season the manager put the following advertisement in the newspapers.

" Opera House, May 24th. All persons that have subscribed, or are willing to subscribe, twenty guineas for an Italian opera to be performed next season under my direction, are desired to send ten guineas to Mr. Drummond,

the banker, who will give them a receipt, and
return the money in case the opera should not
go on.

Signed,   " J. J. HEIDEGGER."

The subscriptions not coming in, no performance took place; and Handel then hired
the theatre of its lessee for the purpose of
bringing out his oratorios. Here were heard
his " Saul," " Alexander's Feast," " Il Trionfo
del Tempo e della Verita," and " Israel in
Egypt." In 1739, the same composer produced his " Jupiter in Argos," a dramatic production, relieved by concertos on the organ;
and in 1740 and the following year, he brought
on the stage of the theatre at Lincoln's Inn,
which he hired for the purpose, three musical
entertainments, — his serenata " Parnasso in
Festa," first produced in 1734, his operetta
" Imeneo," and a musical drama, " Deidamia;"
but the very slight impression they made induced Handel to confine himself entirely to the

production of oratorios. A pasticcio entitled
" Lucio Vero," originally produced in 1716, of
which the chief portion of the music was his,
was performed at the opening of the King's
Theatre in November 1747, and was continued with remarkable success till Christmas,
being the last of nearly fifty operatic productions this fertile writer had presented to the
musical world in England, that were performed
at the Opera House previous to its being
closed in 1750, partly from the want of support,
and in some measure in consequence of the
flight of the manager Dr. Croza, who, not being
more fortunate than his predecessors in office,
made his escape before his speculation had led
him to a prison. Bononcini entered into a
spirited rivalry with Handel; but, talented as
was this composer, he had no chance against
the latter's wonderful resources. Pescetti was
still less successful, and even the genius of
Galuppi could not carry on the contest on anything resembling equal terms. Pergolesi,

Gluck, Paradies, Ciampi, and several other masters of less celebrity, were occasionally re-sorted to, but such of their works as were attempted would not bear comparison with the masterpieces of the sublime Handel. Not-withstanding, however, his extraordinary genius, and the rapidity with with he produced his works, and his continual endeavours to get together a company worthy of performing them, the Italian opera was not heard in England for four years, when the arrival of the cele-brated singer Mingotti led to another attempt to establish it; but even her exertions, assisted by those of the leader of the band, Giardini, an accomplished musician, who shared the ma-nagement with Mingotti, did not meet with sufficient patronage. Signora Mattei and her husband Trombetta, vocalists of considerable reputation, also had the honour of being nearly ruined by the same speculation. The most successful performances at this period were the " Andromaca" of Jomelli, and " Il Filosofo

di Campagna" by Galuppi—productions, the
popularity of which reflect credit upon English
taste.   John Christian Bach arrived in this
country from Italy, where he had deserved and
attained great reputation as a composer, and
was immediately engaged by the manager of
the Italian Opera, in the hope his genius would
support that sinking establishment.   Accordingly, in 1763, he produced his " Orione o sia
Diana Vendicata," and "Zanaida;" and the
remarkable talent they displayed attracted
tolerable though not very productive audiences.
The chief performers after this season were
Signor Manzoli and Signora Scotti.

The opera commenced, in 1765, under the
management of Messrs. Gordon, Vincent, and
Crawford ; but these gentlemen appeared to be
hastening fast to the fate of their predecessors,
when they were saved from ruin for the time
by the production of Piccini's delightful " La
Buona Figliuola."   " La Schiava," by the same
composer, was also singularly successful, but

his other efforts effected no such results. He was succeeded in public favour by the charming Sacchini, and the no less distinguished Anfossi; but their exertions were not more advantageous to the Italian opera in England, than had been those of Handel and Bach; and, again overwhelmed with debts, and suffering from ruinous litigation, that establishment ceased, and was not revived for several years.

It will be seen from what has been stated in these pages, that the patronage extended to foreign music, till after the middle of the last century, was insufficient for the support of an Italian theatre in London. Musical taste, however, was advancing in the best society of the metropolis, and professors of talent were liberally supported as teachers of the harpsichord, violin, and singing. Bach became instructor to the queen, and remained her chamber musician, and a fashionable composer also, till he died in the year 1782. Giardini was supported by many ladies of rank, in whose

houses he, in conjunction with Signora Min-
gotti, frequently gave concerts. The prima
donna and the talented violin-player were on
such occasions assisted by their own pupils,
Mrs. Fox Lane, Lady Milbanke, and Lady
Edgecumbe taking the harpsichord, while Lady
Rockingham, the dowager Lady Carlisle, and
Miss Pelham, exerted their vocal abilities.

Among the other musical entertainments then
in vogue, was the Ridotto, first introduced in this
country in 1722, which consisted of a selection
of songs sung chiefly by Senesino, Baldassari,
Mrs. Anastasia Robinson, and Salvai, after
which the performers on the stage joined the
company in the pit, by passing over a bridge
that connected the two, which was a signal for
the commencement of a ball; this concluded
the amusements of the evening. Ranelagh
Gardens was the original speculation of Mr.
Lacy, a joint patentee with Garrick in Drury
Lane Theatre. They were prettily planned,
extending down to the Thames; a superb

orchestra, from which concerts of vocal and instrumental music were given, was erected in the centre of a capacious rotundo, with boxes for refreshments round the interior, in which part of the company sat, whilst the rest promenaded in full dress before them. At first, the chief vocal pieces performed were oratorio chorusses; but at a rival establishment (Vauxhall) solos for the voice had become so attractive, that it was found necessary to make them a principal feature in the performances at these gardens; and Beard, a celebrated tenor, and Frasi, a singer of considerable talent, were soon heard delighting their frequenters. A display of fireworks concluded the entertainments, which were often closed at an hour that allowed of a late supper being taken at Vauxhall, which in the course of a few years superseded its fashionable rival in the public estimation. At this place Lowe, Reinhold, and Mrs. Arne, were the first vocalists: afterwards Mrs. Weichsell, the mother of Mrs. Billington; In-

cledon, Dignum, Miss Feron, (since Mrs.
Glossop,) Mrs. Bland, and most of the popular
singers of their time, were heard here. For a
considerable period Hook (the father of Theo-
dore Hook, the novelist) composed the Vauxhall
ballads, which were usually the popular songs
of the season. He was succeeded by John
Parry, who, after labouring in his vocation as
industriously as his predecessor, had to make
way for Henry Bishop. These gardens have
also been distinguished for possessing a fine
band, particularly at the latter end of the last
century, when the principal instrumental performers in the kingdom found places in the
orchestra.

Marylebone Gardens, another place of public
resort, of greater antiquity than either Ranelagh or Vauxhall, were first brought into
notice by its musical performances in 1769, at
which period they were purchased by Dr.
Arnold, and having been newly decorated with
considerable taste, were opened to the public

with burlettas and other entertainments, for
which the Doctor composed the music. Concerts were given in Hanover-square as early as
1763, at first by Bach and Abel, and continued
to be a source of attraction for many years
after. Musical entertainments of a similar
nature were held also in commodious rooms
in other parts of the town, and on these occasions every novel performance was sure of at-
tracting a full audience. Of the instrumental
wonders witnessed in the first half of the last
century, a few are worthy of notice. In 1703
Mrs. Champion, a singer of some celebrity, performed for her benefit at Lincoln's Inn Theatre,
the first solo ever publicly heard on the harpsichord. About the same period the first solo of
Corelli heard in England was played on the
violin by Mr. Dean : a few years later, Master
Dubourg, a boy of twelve years of age, exhibited remarkable talent on the same instrument;
and the extraordinary violin performances of
Castrucci delighted the town soon afterwards.

But the great musical marvel of the age was the performance of Mrs. Sarah Ottey on three instruments—the bass-viol, violin, and harpsichord. This was rivalled by Joachim Frederic Creta, on two French horns. The little prodigy, Master Knutzen, at seven years of age, attracted crowds by his performance on the harpsichord; and another juvenile violinist, John Clegg, created no less astonishment. The ability of Caporale and Pasqualino on the violincello; of Guiseppi van Martini, Vincent, and Kytch, on the hautboy; Boston, Wiedeman, and Ballicourt, on the flute; Valentine Snowdon the trumpet; Roseingrave, Greene, Robinson, Magnus, James, Kelway, Keeble, Gladwin, and Stanly, a blind man, on the organ, displayed to the musical world what might be done on their several instruments; and Corbet, the first leader of the opera, did as much to prove to what advantage skilful playing might be cultivated in concerto pieces. These performances were not without producing satisfactory effects upon the lovers of music in England. Several amateurs became celebrated performers, and in some instances composers: as one instance of this, we mention the Earl of Kellie, a violin-player of no ordinary ability, whose overture to the "Maid of the Mill" affords evidence of undoubted talent.

Giardini increased the popularity of the violin, in which object he was ably assisted by Lolli, Pinto, Barthelemon, and Cramer. The viol da gamba found a most skilful player in Charles Frederick Abel; Crosdil and Cervetto were violoncello performers of great celebrity; and Fischer made his hautboy discourse such music, as effaced the impression left upon the public mind by his predecessors. While such attention was paid to the orchestra, the voice was cultivated with equal care. The principal foreign singers met with talented pupils, who were afterwards found acquisitions to the English stage, and in some instances to the Italian also. A few of the most distin-

guished vocalists of the Italian opera, by acquiring a knowledge of the English language,
were enabled to obtain considerable popularity
as singers of English songs. They assisted at
oratorios, appeared at some of the English
theatres, and were usually the chief attraction
at public concerts. In this state of things
another attempt was made to establish an
Italian opera in this country, which was commenced under favourable auspices, with the
arrival of Rubinelli and Mara, who first appeared in London in the season of 1786, in the
opera of " Virginia," composed by Tarchi.
Madame Mara had sung for two or three years
previously at a series of concerts which had
been given every season at the Pantheon in
Oxford street; but in the opera she had more
scope for the display of her fine voice, and
there made a very powerful impression. Signor
Rubinelli succeeded Pacchierotti, who had been
almost as much admired by the ladies as his
more celebrated countryman, Farinelli. He

was equally efficient as a singer and as an actor, and for several years was the chief male attraction at the King's Theatre, the oratorios, and the principal public and private concerts.

Mara had not long enjoyed her celebrity as a prima donna without finding it threatened by powerful rivals, in the persons of Signora Storace and Mrs. Billington. Storace made her first appearance at the King's Theatre with Signor Borelli, a basso of remarkable talent, in Paesiello's comic opera, " Gli Schiavi per Amore," in which she established her reputation. Billington had made a name for herself, as a singer of English operatic music, on the stage, at the concert and the oratorio, wherein she distinguished herself above every competitor, till she left this country on a visit to Italy, where she stayed six years, and returned so improved, that Storace, who during that time had succeeded her on the English stage with an effect that no other singer had produced there, found her popularity affected by her re-appearance. She was not engaged at the King's Theatre, at which her brother, Mr. Weichsell, was leader, till the season of 1802, when she made her first appearance on that stage, on the 4th of December, in Nasolini's serious opera " Merope," wherein she produced such effect as secured her re-engagement the following season, and her unrivalled popularity as long as her voice lasted.

Although we had almost every season a new prima donna, not one attracted sufficient attention to be considered formidable to Mara, Storace, or Billington, till Madame Banti made her appearance on the 26th of April, 1794, in Bianchi's opera, " Semiramide, o la vendetta di Nino." The reputation this accomplished singer had acquired in Italy had preceded her into England, but her performance proved that her merits had not been exaggerated. She was equally admirable in the bravura as in the cantabile; possessed a voice remarkable for its sweetness, power, and flexibility, and was a

graceful actress.   She soon became fashionable,
and the next season repeated her personification
of the same character, having Michael Kelly as
a coadjutor, who on that occasion made his bow
to an Italian opera audience.   Her fine singing and acting, aided by the operatic talents of
Viganoni, Benelli, and Morelli, attracted such
excellent houses at the King's Theatre, that at
this period (about the close of the last century)
the Italian opera might at last be said to have
been established in England.

Music now began to be very generally cultivated in the higher circles.   Concerts were
held at the houses of several of the principal
nobility, in which many of them assisted.   The
Prince of Wales and the Duke of Gloucester
were performers on the violoncello, and the
Duke of Cumberland on the violin, and they
frequently joined the private orchestra at Carl-
ton Palace, and at Lord Hampden's.   The
Duke of Queensberry and Lord Boyle were
also liberal patrons of music.   The professional

concerts were well attended, especially those of Salomon, which introduced into this country many distinguished musicians. On the violin, Salomon, Jarnovicki, and Viotti; on the piano, Schroeter, Pleyel, Clementi, and Dussek, were the most celebrated. Madame Gautherot, from Paris, also came forward as a violin-player, and it has been asserted that she was the first female who attempted a concerto on that instrument before an English audience; but she was preceded twenty years before by Madame Syrmen, whose performances excited great astonishment, as well as by Mrs. Sarah Ottey, mentioned in a previous page. Florio and Graeff were the principal flute-players about the conclusion of the last century; Schwartz and Holmes on the bassoon, Mahon on the clarionet, Sarjent on the trumpet, and Stamotz and Shield on the tenor.

The taste of the musical public had undergone a considerable change during the last half of the eighteenth century. Handel was still

popular, but only in his oratorios or concertos.*
Bononcini was listened to no more in an entire
opera. The harpsichord lessons of Domenico
Scarlatti, Alberto, and Paradies, had made way
for the piano-forte sonatas of Haydn, Pleyel,
and Dussek. The operas performed at the
King's Theatre were usually selected from the
works of Cimarosa, Gluck, Paesiello, Sarti,
Sacchini, and Winter; which having the advantage of a fine orchestra and a company of
vocalists, the best the continent could supply,
rarely failed of exciting intense admiration. By
these judicious performances the Italian opera
in England became so fashionable in this
country, that in the higher circles a box at the
opera was thought as necessary as a residence
in town.

* An attempt was made at the King's Theatre, in 1787, by
Dr. Arnold, to make Handel's operatic music fashionable, by a
selection of that master's productions, introduced in an opera
called " Giulio Cesare in Egitto ;" but, even with the assistance of Mara and Rubinelli, it was only heard a few nights.

Madame Banti was retained as a favourite, notwithstanding that, besides being obliged to maintain a contest with Mara, Storace, and Billington, she found rivals in Madame Morichelli and Madame Bolla, and in fact in every prima donna that made a successful appearance at the King's Theatre. She at last was forced to make way for Mrs. Billington, who was so much the idol of the musical public as to eclipse every competitor, till the arrival of the celebrated Grassini. It may be in the remembrance of veteran frequenters of the opera, the appearance of these accomplished singers in 1804, in Winter's opera, " Il ratto di Proserpine," and how exquisitely their fine voices harmonised in the pathetic duo in the second act. Grassini showed herself an admirable actress and a most expressive singer. Her voice was of a very rich quality, and she employed it with the talent of a superior musician. Viganoni was associated with them in the same opera, and the effect produced by them in the terzetto

"Mi lasci" was a musical treat of exceeding rarity. The following season these celebrated singers were assisted by Storace, Morelli, and Braham, it being the first appearance of the latter gentleman at the King's Theatre; and the style in which they sang the music of Martini's beautiful opera "La Cosa Rara," proved a source of the greatest gratification to the subscribers. Braham was much admired. He had previously gained a well-deserved celebrity by his performances in several English operas at Covent Garden, and by singing at concerts and oratorios; and the manner in which he acquitted himself on this occasion led to his re-engagement.

At this period Madame Catalani was creating on the continent the great celebrity by which she for many years afterwards became distinguished, and such marvellous accounts of her execution had preceded her into this country, that when she made her début at the King's Theatre, in Portagallo's grand serious opera,

"Semiramide," the house was crowded to an excess never before known. Her rich, powerful, and flexible organ, and her easy yet brilliant vocalization, excited the most enthusiastic applause, and by the time she advertised her benefit in the following season, wherein she performed the first act of the serious opera, " La Morte di Mithridate," and afterwards with the same brilliant success appeared in the first act in the comic " Il Fanatico per la Musica," she had displaced Mrs. Billington as the reigning favourite. Her popularity now became immense. She was the first singer called on to sing one song three times, which occurred during her performance in the Italian comic opera, " La Freschetana." Her success spoiled her. She became arrogant and capricious, and exacted for her engagements terms unparalleled in the annals of foreign extortion. In this, however, it is but just to say she was much exceeded by some of her successors.

The first prima donna who made any de-

cided impression after Catalani was Madame
Bertinotti Radicati, who made her début, in
1810, in the serious opera, "Zaira. She was
ably assisted by Signor Trammezzani, a talented
singer, who performed in comic and serious
characters with equal ability; but Catalani still
maintained her supremacy. In 1813, the
latter was associated at the opera for the first
time with Mrs. Dickons, (previously of considerable celebrity as Miss Poole,) who played
the Countess in Mozart's comic opera, "Le
Nozze di Figaro," to Catalani's Susannah, with
admirable effect. They were both re-engaged
the following season, which was distinguished
also by the return of Grassini, who was most
rapturously received. No very important new
engagement was made after this in the Italian
company till the arrival of Madame Fodor,
who made her first appearance, in 1816, in
Paer's "Griselda," wherein she produced great
effect, particularly in the air "Griselda Sa-
reggio." Naldi, an excellent baritone, who

made his début, as far back as 1806, in Gu-
glielmi's comic opera, "Le Due Nozzo ed un
Marito," was also greatly applauded in the
same opera. Fodor acted with Braham, when
the season was more advanced, with equal
success, in "La Clemenzo di Tito," and was
re-engaged the following season. This year
is a remarkable one in the annals of the
opera, as it boasts the introduction to the
English public of Madame Pasta, Madame
Camporese, Signor Crevelli, and Signor Ambrogetti. Of these, the three first commenced
their career at the King's Theatre in Cimarosa's grand serious opera "Penelope," being
its earliest performance in England. The expression of Pasta, her splendid vocalization, and
fine acting, were instantly recognised; due
justice was also done to the graceful singing of
Camporese, and the taste exemplified in Crevelli's management of a tenor voice of considerable power and compass. But they were
heard to most advantage in "Le Nozze de

Figaro," in which Ambrogetti appeared as the Count; Fodor as the Countess; Camporese as Susanna; Pasta as the Page; and Naldi as Figaro. So brilliant a cast has rarely been met with; and with a result equally favourable they performed together, on the 12th of the following April, in another splendid opera of Mozart, " Il Don Giovanni."

Pasta's impersonations were considered as the finest things of the kind ever seen in England—those of a tragic character especially. Her Medea, her Desdemona, her Tancredi, and Romeo, were masterpieces of acting. Ambrogetti was also a distinguished actor. Who that has ever enjoyed it, can forget his thrilling performance in the serious opera, " L'Agnese?" It has been stated that, before he attempted it, he visited Bedlam, and, from the maniacs there confined, drew the extraordinary picture of a madman he represented on the stage. This celebrated production of Paer's we have only seen once performed since, and

that was within the last five or six years, for
the benefit of Tamburini, who played the principal character well, but not with the effect of
his predecessor. Crevelli did not retain his
place on the boards of the King's Theatre; he
soon afterwards commenced as a teacher of
singing in London, which he still remains.

In the summer of 1818, Signor Garcia, the
father of Malibran, made his début on this stage,
on the occasion of the first performance of Rossini's very popular "Il Barbiere di Seviglia," in
which he acquitted himself with great credit, both
as a singer and as an actor. He had a tenor voice
of excellent quality, which he displayed to particular advantage in the music of this charming
opera. In the following year he repeated the
character (Conte d'Almaviva) to the Figaro of
Placci, the Rosina of Madame Georgia Bellochi, and the Don Bartolo of Ambrogetti, with
increased popularity. It was the first season
of Bellochi and Placci; the former possessed a
fine soprano, and the latter a baritone of a

remarkably rich tone; and the singing of both afforded the utmost satisfaction. Madame Ronzi de Begnis, and Signor de Begnis, in 1821, succeeded them, and the delicacy of the lady's voice, and the buffo qualities of the gentleman, were much approved of for a season or two. Signora Caradori joined the company the following year, and her sweet voice and finished style found numerous admirers. Her first character in England was that of the Page, in "Le Nozze di Figaro." Garcia was still engaged here in 1823, and particularly distinguished himself in the "Ricciardo e Zoraido;" the beautiful trio, as sung by him, Camporese, and Madame Vestris, who had already obtained considerable reputation as an operatic singer, elicited an unanimous encore.

One of the great attractions of the following season was Madame Colbran Rossini, the wife of the celebrated composer, (who had just been engaged as director and composer of the theatre;) but, though possessed of considerable

advantages both in person and talent, she suffered by a comparison with Catalani and Pasta,
who performed during the same period.   In the
summer of 1825, the lovers of music in England
were advertised of the first introduction to
them of a quality of voice which must have
been strange to most of their ears, and some of
the public journals went so far as to denounce
the exhibition; notwithstanding which, Signor
Velluti was favourably heard at the King's
Theatre in Meyerbeer's " Il Crociato in Egitto,"
in the part of Armando, which had been
written expressly for him, in which opera he
was ably assisted by a young débutante, of extraordinary promise, in the character of Felicia,
This was MARIA FELICIA GARCIA, the subject
of these volumes.

By this time musical taste in this country
had made prodigious advances; for, since the
commencement of the present century, some of
the finest compositions ever written were produced at the King's Theatre, and executed by

vocal and instrumental performers capable of
doing them justice. Their popularity in
England is an undoubted proof of the progress
of English taste. Of these operas, we have to
notice the masterpieces of Mozart and Rossini,
which speedily became established favourites,
and seem to obtain increased admiration at
every repetition. The richness of their instru-
mentation, the beauty of their vocal solos, and
the no less delightful character of their harmonised pieces, combined to effect a degree of
intellectual gratification, which, it may safely
be asserted, no art but music could have produced. We cannot with such certainty compliment the subscribers to the Italian opera
on their improvement in musical taste since
then. They appear too much enamoured of
Donizetti, and other composers of the same
unoriginal character—writers rather of *solfeggi*
than music. In other respects, the performances at the King's Theatre, and the crowded
audiences they attract, indicate a much more

reputable judgment. Grisi has almost reconciled us to the loss of Malibran—Lablache
rivals the achievements of Farinelli, and Rubini
has excelled all his predecessors. Instrumental players have arrived at a similar perfection; the last century brought forth nothing
like the performances of Paganini on the violin,
Lindley on the violoncello, Bochsa on the harp,
and Thalberg on the piano; and vocal and
orchestral music are cultivated to an extent and
with a success in England never previously
known.

MEMOIRS OF

MADAME MALIBRAN,

BY

THE COUNTESS DE MERLIN.

MEMOIRS, &c.

CHAPTER I.

Manuel Garcia, the father of Madame Malibran—His talent as an actor and singer—He quits Spain and proceeds to France and Italy—His performance at the Opera in Paris—Commencement of Maria Garcia's musical studies—Her voice and intonation—Garcia's severity in the instruction of his daughter—Maria's fear of her father's displeasure.

MARIA GARCIA was born in Paris, in the year 1808. Her father, Manuel Garcia, was a Spaniard, and was for many years a popular actor and singer at the Prince's Theatre at Madrid.

Conscious, however, that his musical education
was imperfect, and that he had within him the
germ of something greater than had yet been
shown, he left Spain, and visited Paris, where
his daughter was born. From Paris he proceeded to Italy, and after a few years' study he
returned to the French capital, where his great
talent was acknowledged by the most unqualified
applause. His performances of Count Almaviva,
of Otello, and Don Giovanni, will never be
forgotten by those who witnessed them.

Garcia devoted himself to his musical studies
with the most energetic perseverance, and in a
short time he commenced the musical education
of his daughter. The violence and irritability
of his temper, joined to the energy with which
he himself surmounted the difficulties of musical
study, rendered him anything but an easy task-
master.

Maria Garcia's first years of practice were
painful and tedious. Nothing short of that
firmness of character, with which nature had so

liberally endowed her, could have made her a musician. Her aptitude for musical study was but slowly developed, and her voice wanted flexibility; yet, in spite of all these disadvantages, she resolutely persevered, and she overcame each fresh difficulty with increasing courage. Some credit is doubtless due to her father: he never allowed the plea of "I cannot" to prevail. In his opinion the determination to conquer difficulties was sufficient; he admitted of no excuse, no apology. To resolve was to do; to fail was want of perseverance.

Maria Garcia's voice was at first feeble. The lower tones were harsh and imperfectly developed, the upper tones were indifferent in quality, and limited in extent, and the middle tones wanted clearness. Her intonation was so false as to warrant the apprehension that her ear was defective. I have often heard her say that at the commencement of her vocal practice she would sometimes sing so much out of tune that her father in despair would leave the piano and retire to another part of the house. Maria, then a mere child, would hurry after him, and with tears implore him to renew the lesson. " Did you hear how much you were out of tune ?" Garcia would say. " O yes, papa." " Well, then, let us begin again." This serves to show that Garcia's severity was modified by the consideration of the possible; and that he felt how insufficient is even the most resolute determination in the effort to overcome certain organic defects.

One evening Maria and I were practising a duet into which Garcia had introduced some embellishments. Maria, who was then about fourteen years of age, was vainly endeavouring to execute a certain passage, and at last uttered the words " I cannot." In an instant the Andalusian blood of her father rose. He fixed his large eyes sternly upon her and said, " Did I hear aright ?" In another instant she sang the passage perfectly. When we were alone, I expressed my surprise at this. " O !" cried she, clasping her hands with emotion, " such is the effect of an angry look from my father, that I am sure it would make me jump from the roof of the house without hurting myself."

CHAPTER II.

Contrast between Madame Malibran's feeble health and strong mental power—Her ardent temperament—Her self-denial, generosity, and charity—The unreserved frankness of her disposition—Difference between Maria Garcia and her sister Pauline—Promising talents of Pauline—Madame Malibran's performance of Desdemona—Effect she produced in the celebrated romance—Her power of sustaining the tones of her voice amidst the strongest excitement of feeling—Cause to which she assigned the acquisition of that power.

DURING her early years Maria Garcia showed symptoms of that delicacy of health which characterised her after life. Long ere she reached womanhood her spirit would struggle against her physical strength, rather than she would give up a difficulty, or allow it to be beyond her power to conquer. She would frequently swoon when overcome by the violent conflict which ever raged within her—the struggle between the mental energy and the delicate constitution with which nature had endowed her. Whilst suffering to her utmost powers of endurance, and struggling against pain and debility, this inimitable songstress has often won her brightest laurels.

Her impassioned and ardent feeling sometimes betrayed her into violent paroxysms of temper; but even on those occasions it was easy to soothe her by an appeal to her kindness and generosity; the voice of friendship, even in reproof, was hearkened to, and its counsels followed. She was ever ready to confess her error, to solicit pardon, and to atone for any injury she might have inflicted; in short, she made friends of all who knew her.

Madame Malibran has been accused of being avaricious and penurious. As far as concerned her own gratifications, she was so. Brought up in a rigid school, with the example of her parents before her, she never indulged in those expenses and luxuries common to females in the theatrical profession. Her life was one of self-denial. On herself she never threw away money; but, on the other hand, who that ever sought and needed her assistance, had cause to accuse her of avarice? Who can say she was uncharitable? Her whole income was at the disposal of others—her purse was ever open to the needy and deserving.

The unreserved frankness of her nature imparted a certain degree of *brusquerie* to her manners, especially in her professional intercourse. She was totally devoid of that sort of diplomatic disguise indispensable in certain dependent conditions. Her greatest fault was her inability to disguise her feelings. Though a first-rate actress on the stage, yet a child might read her thoughts when in her private and domestic character.

There is a painful necessity in the life of an

artist; viz. that of surrendering his judgment to
the opinions of others. In this respect, the most
celebrated actor or actress that ever trod the stage
is a slave. The success or failure of an actor or
singer often depends upon the mere caprice of
an audience, whose wayward humour makes or
mars the fate of talent. The feelings of a
debutante should therefore be well schooled, ere
she appears before the public. One day I
made this remark to Garcia, and added a slight
reproach on his severe treatment of one so
likely to have much to suffer. " I am aware,"
replied he, " that the world blames me; but I am
right. Maria can never become great but at
this price: her proud and stubborn spirit requires a hand of iron to control it. Towards
her younger sister, on the contrary, I have never
had cause to exercise harshness, and yet she
will make her way.* This is the difference:

* Pauline, though only seventeen years of age, promises
to become an ornament to the stage, and a worthy successor
to her talented and lamented sister.

the one requires to be bound by a chain, the other may be led by a silken thread." Such was the opinion of Garcia, who, in accordance with these notions, made his daughter pay dearly in her youth for the triumphs of her maturer years.

Everybody knows how admirably Maria Malibran sang the romance in the third act of Otello. Who can forget her tears, and the melancholy expression with which she addressed to Emilia the words, " Ricevi dei labri dell' amica il baccio estremo;" it was truly sublime.

One evening I occupied the stage-box during this performance. My whole soul was with her; I gazed on her with the deepest interest. I was entranced and overcome by the spell of the fascinating being before me. On our return home after the play, I asked her how she could sing so well under so strong an excitement of feeling—how she could manage her voice whilst her eyes were streaming with tears? She naïvely answered, " It is not the result of study; I never practised this as an art. In my younger years, I have often found my eyes suffused with tears, whilst singing behind my father's chair, and I have been afraid he should perceive me weeping. I therefore exerted every endeavour to form my notes correctly, fearing he might chide me for my folly. I have often sang while tears flowed down my cheeks." Thus the severity of Garcia lent its aid to improve those extraordinary talents with which nature had endowed her. Her girlish sorrows gave her a power possessed by no other living singer : a power which has often wreathed her brows with crowns of triumph, and called forth the admiration and surprise of thousands.

CHAPTER III.

Madame Malibran's talent for drawing—Her caricatures—
Needle-work—Her power of conversing in various languages—Incongruities in her disposition and manner—Her
disregard of flattery—Her difficult musical exercises—Severe
routine of study requisite for a public singer.

Madame Malibran's facility in acquiring any
accomplishment to which she applied her talent
was truly extraordinary. She conquered difficulties which others would fear to encounter. Although her father strictly confined her attention
to singing, yet she, at the same time, and, as it
were, without effort, cultivated other accom-
plishments. She was a first-rate pianiste; and
though she never had a master to instruct her in

the art, yet she evinced exquisite talent for drawing—her caricatures were admirable. She never saw any fancy work, any sort of embroidery, or other needlework, that she could not instantly imitate, and often surpass. Her theatrical costumes were invariably the creation of her own fancy, and in many instances were actually made by herself. I have frequently seen her engaged at needlework whilst she was practising her singing; her stitches being as delicate as her notes. She could write and speak four or five languages with perfect facility; and I have heard her, in a mixed company, maintain a conversation with various individuals, speaking to each in a different language.

The disposition of Maria Malibran presented the strangest incongruities. She united in herself strength of mind and credulity, resolution and weakness. When elated to the highest pitch, the following instant would reduce her to the deepest despondency. She was generous to excess, mean in trifles; bold, yet timid, alternately sublime and childish.

Maria appeared to have imbibed from the various classes in which she had mingled their various manners. She had received, from the different countries she had visited during her years of travel, impressions from each, which, strangely blended in her mind, often made her seem capricious and inconsistent.

She had a way, peculiar to herself, of creating friends. She spurned the ordinary road to the heart; she despised flattery herself, and never addressed it to others. It was not by insinuating manners that she won the good graces of those whose suffrage she sought. No; it was by bold eccentricity and originality, by candour, sometimes verging on unpoliteness. By the habit of freely expressing her feelings, she commanded and secured the love of all who knew her.

In her childhood, her father often made her sing before his friends, canons and nocturnes

of his own composition, being naturally anxious
to give proof of her talents. But in later years
he never permitted this: he strictly confined
her practice to musical exercises—exercises the
most dry, tedious, and laborious that can be
imagined. How few can form any idea of the
toil to which the young singer must be subjected,
ere she can attain any degree of perfection in
public performance; how few would envy the
crown of glory so painfully earned!

CHAPTER IV.

Garcia's method of instruction—Grassini, Pizzaroni, Pasta, &c.
—Importance of the correct mode of exercising the voice—
Garcia's remark on this subject—Defects of the old French
school of singing—Method of practice for equalising the
different parts of the voice—Requisite exercises for soprano
voices—Extempore exercises practised by Garcia's pupils —
Importance attached by Garcia to the practice of *Solfeggi*.

GARCIA's method of teaching singing was formed
on the excellent model of those old musicians,
the traces of whose style are daily vanishing
even in Italy. This system did not consist in
directing the practice of the pupil to a variety
of *fiorituri*, which, like the fashions of the day,
enjoy an evanescent favour, and are soon for-

gotten. Garcia's system of instruction was founded on principles whose superiority has been acknowledged in all ages of the musical art; those principles which have been studied by Grassini, Colbrand, Pizzaroni, Pasta, and other distinguished ornaments of the Italian scene. To these principles, seconded by high intelligence in their application, we are indebted to the most brilliant talent that has shed lustre on the musical drama of the present day—the talent of Maria Malibran.

The first objects to which the young singer should direct attention are—to equalise what may be termed the instrument of the voice, by correcting those imperfections from which even the finest organ is not exempt;—to augment the number of tones by constant and careful practice;*—to draw breath quietly and without

* Garcia used to say, " Those who wish to sing well should not practise without knowing how to practise. It is only by earning the secret of practising well that there is any possibility of learning to sing well,"

hurry ;—to prepare the throat for emitting the
tone with clearness and purity, swelling the
note gradually but boldly, so as to develope the
utmost power of the voice, and finally to blend
the notes in such a manner that each may be
heard distinctly, but not abruptly.   But, on the
other hand, it is requisite to guard against a
false application of this principle, lest the
student should fall into the defects of the old
French method, by which one note was allowed
to die away with a false expression of languid
tenderness, and to fall, as it were, *en defaillance*
on the succeeding tone.   To blend the tones of
the voice according to the best Italian method,
the note should first be emitted in a *straight
line,* (to employ a figurative expression,) and
then form a curve, the intermediate tones being
given merely by sympathetic vibration, and the
voice should again fall on the required note
with decision and clearness.＊

＊ It is very difficult to give a perfectly clear and satisfactory
explanation of the operations of a mechanism, the hidden mo-

Whatever be the quality of the voice, the singer should take especial care of the upper notes, and avoid too much practice upon them, for that part of the voice being most delicate, its quality is most easily injured. On the contrary, by practising more particularly on the middle and lower notes, they acquire strength, and an important object is gained, (which is in strict accordance with one of the essential principles of acoustics,) namely, that of making the grave tones strike the ear with the same degree of force as the acute tones.

To the adoption of this rational rule is to be ascribed the great superiority of the Italian

tion of which can only be guessed at from the vague observations of singers themselves. .All conclusions, therefore, respecting the phenomena of the voice, must be drawn from very obscure sources. All persons, except singers, must regard these conclusions as mere metaphysical obscurities, and even to the majority of those who practise the art of singing, the management of the voice is rather the result of mechanical dexterity than of observation or reasoning.

to the French school of singing. By softening
the upper tones, and giving strength to the
lower and middle tones, either by dint of
the accent of the voice, or the accent proper
to the words, the ear is never offended, and the
music penetrates to the soul of the hearer
without any of that harshness which shocks and
irritates the nerves. In like manner the demi-
tints in a beautiful picture, by blending the
colours one with another, charm the eye by
producing a vague appearance of reality.

Exercises for strengthening the low and
middle notes of the voice are more important
for sopranos than for voices of any other class;
first, because, in general, that part of the voice
is most feeble; and next, because the transition
from the *voce di petto* to the *voce di testa* tends
to deteriorate the purity of some tones, and to
impart a feebler, or, if I may so express myself,
a *stifled* effect to others. It is, therefore, requisite to keep up a continual practice of the
defective note with the pure note which follows

or precedes it, in order to obtain a perfect uniformity in their quality. This practice was one of the greatest difficulties which Maria Garcia had to surmount, the lower notes of her voice being strong and well toned, whilst the notes of transition were feeble and husky.

One important point in this method is the secret of developing the *voce di petto* in soprano voices. Garcia was convinced that breast tones existed in all voices of that class, but that the only difficulty consisted in the art of developing them.

In proportion as the voice of the pupil improved, it was Garcia's custom to prescribe exercises more and more difficult until every obstacle was surmounted; but he rarely noted down a set passage for his pupils. His method was to strike a chord on the piano, and to say to them, " Now sing any passage you please;" and he would make them execute a passage in this way ten or twenty times in succession. The result was, that the pupil sang precisely

that which was suited to his voice, and suggested by his taste. Solfeggi exercises, performed in this way, presented a character of
individuality, being suggested by the feeling of
the moment. Another advantage of this mode
of practice was, that the pupil gained a perfect
mastery over his voice by dint of exercising his
own inspirations, and that he was at liberty to
follow the dictates of his own taste without
fear or hesitation.

Garcia never permitted his pupils, whilst they
were in the course of tuition, to sing vocal
compositions with words: he confined them
strictly to Solfeggi. But when he considered
any one of them sufficiently advanced he would
say, " Now you are a singer; you may try
anything you please—like a child out of leading-
strings, you can *run alone.*" It may be added,
that Garcia invariably applied his principles
most rigorously to those pupils on whom he
founded the highest hopes.

CHAPTER V.

Maria Garcia's first appearance in public—Rossini's arrival in Paris—His *Siege of Corinth* and *William Tell*—Revolution in musical taste—Nuptial cantata—Amateur performance—Bordogni and Isabel—Impressions produced by Maria Garcia's first public performance.

MARIA GARCIA was only fifteen years of age when a circumstance occurred which led to her first appearance in public, and to the first developement of that talent which at a subsequent period of her life rendered her so celebrated.

Rossini had just arrived in Paris. His arrival formed an epoch in the musical annals of the French capital. But though his principal compositions were already well known and duly appreciated in France, yet, in that country the genius of song still slumbered. Rossini appeared, and composed his *Siege of Corinth* and *Guillaume Tell*. These operas produced a total change in the style of vocal execution among the French.

A short time before he quitted Italy, Rossini had composed a nuptial cantata in honour of the marriage of my relative, M. de Penalver. This cantata, which consisted of four vocal parts, had never been heard in a complete form, not even with the piano-forte accompaniment. M. de Penalver, who happened to be in Paris at the time here alluded to, felt a desire to hear the piece with the full instrumental accompaniments. He expressed this wish to Rossini, with whom I was not then acquainted, adding that he should like me to take a part in the performance. The *Maestro*, who had a prejudice against amateur performances, coolly replied, " No, no, my dear sir, that must not be : I have just arrived in Paris," added he with a smile, and you would have me commence with a *fiasco*. We will, if you please, get Isabel and Garcia to try the cantata with the piano-forte accompaniment: that will afford you an idea of it. M. Penalver urged him to accede to his wish; but all that he could obtain was Rossini's consent to hear me sing on the following day. The trial was made, and Rossini declared his willingness to have the piece performed with the full accompaniments. The orchestra was complete: wind instruments, drums, triangles—nothing was wanting; and the company was so numerous, that I was obliged to have my drawing-room doors taken off the hinges. The parts for the tenor and bass voices were assigned to Bordogni and Pelligrini; but we knew not where to find a contralto. In the midst of our embarrasment, Garcia, who had hitherto concealed the talent of his daughter, as a miser would hide a treasure, proposed that she should take the part.

At that time Maria's voice had attained a

considerable degree of perfection. Her *voce di petto* possessed all that power which subsequently excited such admiration, but the other parts of her voice were still harsh and husky; there was an obvious conflict of art against nature. In this, which may be termed her first public performance, Maria Garcia maintained a perfect self-possession. She manifested not the least trace of timidity. It seemed as though she felt a secret conviction of her future success, and that this presentiment, combined with a consciousness of the necessity of exertion, inspired her with that confidence indispensable to all whose talents are an object of public suffrage. To insure success in art, a just confidence in one's own resources is not less necessary than superior talent.

CHAPTER VI.

FROM Paris Garcia proceeded with his family to London, where his daughter mode her *debút* at the King's Theatre. One of her early performances was marked by an amusing incident: it serves to show the laudable ambition which animated the young singer, and the

c 2

courage with which she encountered difficulties
at the very outset of her career. She had to
sing with Velluti a duo in Zingarelli's *Romeo e
Giulietta.* In the morning they rehearsed it
together, and at that rehearsal, as at all preceding ones, Velluti, like an experienced stager,
sang the plain notes of his part, reserving his
fiorituri for the evening, in the fear that the
young debutante would imitate them. Accordingly, at the evening performance, Velluti sang
his solo part, interspersing it with the most
florid ornaments, and closing it with a new
and brilliant cadence, which quite enchanted the
audience. The *musico* cast a glance of mingled
triumph and pity on poor Maria, as she advanced to the stage-lamps. What was the
astonishment of the audience to hear her execute the ornaments of Velluti, imparting to
them even additional grace, and crowning her
triumph with a bold and superb improvisation.
Amidst the torrent of applause which followed
this effort, and whilst trembling from the ex-

citement it occasioned, Maria felt her arm
rudely grasped as it were by a hand of iron.
Immediately the word " *Briccona !*" pronounced
in a suppressed and angry tone by Velluti,
afforded her a convincing proof that every triumph carries with it its mortification.

I do not believe there is any living singer
capable of venturing on a *tour de force* similar
to that performed by Maria Garcia on this occasion. She was, at the time of her first
appearance at the King's Theatre, only sixteen
years of age.

Garcia next engaged himself and his family
to perform at New York, and in consequence
they all left England for America. Maria took
the principal parts in several of Rossini's operas,
and excited great admiration. She was particularly successful in *Desdemona* and *Cenerentola*,
though the parts are so different from each
other. The principal individuals of the American operatic company were Garcia, his daughter, his wife, and son ; the others were merely

feeble auxiliaries. It was amusing to hear Maria describe the pains she took to make singers of performers who had no requisites for singing — not even voices. But, in spite of every obstacle, the performances were well got up.

Shortly after Garcia's arrival in America, M. Malibran, a French merchant established at New York, solicited the hand of Maria. Garcia refused his consent; but Maria, young as she was, began already to feel weary of her laborious public life and her filial dependence. She rejoiced at the idea of emancipating herself, and, in her girlish inexperience, little thought that, in breaking the parental chain, she would bind herself in fetters heavier and more lasting. She did not reflect that the soul of the artist, imbued with the fire of genius, can never relinquish the exercise of that art for which nature has fitted it, and that the hardest filial dependence is nevertheless the sweetest of all dependences. As we wander onward in the

journey of life, we all look back with affection
and regard to the paternal home.

Garcia's temper created great unhappiness in
his family. Madame Garcia, mild and gentle
as an angel of peace, vainly strove to soothe the
violence of her husband; but he became more and
more violent and irritable. One evening Otello
was to be performed: Garcia, who had been
much out of humour during the day, was to play
the part of the Moor, and his daughter that of
Desdemona. In the scene in which Otello seizes
Desdemona for the purpose of stabbing her,
Maria perceived that the dagger which her
father held in his hand was a real instrument of
death, and not one of those sham weapons
used by actors. Maria immediately recognised the dagger which her father brandished
furiously in his hand. It was one which Garcia
had purchased from a Turk a few days previously, and, at the time he bought it, he had
remarked the peculiar sharpness of the blade.
Maria beheld the deadly weapon approach her

bosom, and, frantic with terror, she uttered the
words, " *Papa! Papa! por Dios no me
mates!* " * Poor Maria's terror, as may readily
be supposed, was unfounded. Garcia had no
intention of murdering his daughter. The fact
was, that the stage-dagger being mislaid, he
merely made use of his own as a substitute
for it.

When Madame Malibran related to me this
anecdote, I inquired what the audience thought
of her strange exclamation. " Oh! replied
she, " no one seemed to be aware that
anything extraordinary had occurred. My
terror appeared to be nothing more than what
was incidental to my part; and as to my speaking Spanish, no one had the least suspicion
that it was not very good Italian."

* " Papa! papa! for Heaven's sake do not kill me! "

CHAPTER VII.

Maria Garcia's marriage—M. Malibran's bankruptcy—Garcia
leaves the United States, and proceeds to Mexico—Noble
exertions of Madame Malibran—She studies English singing—Her success on the American stage—Her generous
endeavours to relieve her husband—She leaves America and
returns to Europe—Her arrival in Paris—Renews her acquaintance with the authoress of these Memoirs—Favourable impression produced by her first visit—Anticipations
of her success—The musical jury—The unbelievers converted.

M. MALIBRAN made brilliant promises to Garcia's family. Maria strongly urged her father
to consent to the marriage, and at length it was
concluded. In a few weeks after this event M.
Malibran became a bankrupt, before he had
performed the promises he held out to his wife's

family. This event exasperated to the utmost
degree the violence of Garcia's temper. In the
fear that he might be driven to some act of
desperation, he was prevailed upon to leave the
United States. He proceeded to Mexico with
all his family, except Maria. She, on awaking
from the brilliant dreams in which she had
been nursed since her marriage, found herself
in a foreign land, separated from her parents,
and united to a man who was unable to protect
her, and who, being deprived of the means of
existence, had no resource but in the talents of
his wife.

Maria Malibran was endued with that energy
of character which rendered her capable of
the noblest exertions. After the departure of
Garcia and his family, the Italian company at
New York was broken up. Madame Malibran
immediately commenced the study of English
vocal music, and made her appearance on the
national stage.

What indefatigable patience, what active in-

telligence, were required to surmount the numerous difficulties which presented themselves to
her at every step! What mental courage she
must have summoned to subdue the perturbation
of spirit and the embarrassment attendant on
her fallen circumstances! Regarding her husband's bankruptcy merely as his misfortune, she
thought only of soothing his distress. Her
generous heart, which was always exalted to
enthusiasm by the consciousness of doing good,
enabled her to brave every obstacle. She succeeded beyond her hopes, and every evening a
considerable sum of money was paid by the
manager of the theatre to M. Malibran for his
wife, who, in order to render the fruit of her exertions effectual, had entered into an agreement
that her salary should be paid nightly.

Notwithstanding her brilliant success in
America, imperative reasons induced M. Malibran to send his wife to Europe, and it was
agreed that she should there resume her exer-

tions, and remit to him the emoluments derived from them.

Madame Malibran had not yet completed her twentieth year when she arrived in Paris. This was in December 1827. She went to reside with her husband's sister.

Though a native of Paris, yet the seclusion which her studies imposed on her had prevented her from forming any acquaintances during her previous residence in the French capital; consequently, on her return, after a few years' absence, she found herself completely desolate. A recollection of the regard I had cherished for her in her girlhood induced her to come to me.

This interesting young creature, a wanderer from a distant land, presented herself to me. Her dark silken hair hung in long ringlets on her neck, and she was simply attired in a dress of white muslin. Her youth, her beauty, her intelligence, her friendless and destitute condition, all combined to excite my deepest interest. I gazed on her with mingled feelings of sympathy and admiration. She seated herself at the piano, and I was charmed with her performance.

She expressed a wish to sing a duet with me, but she had not sung many bars, when suddenly stopping, and throwing her arms round my neck, she exclaimed, " O ! how this reminds me of the time when we used to practise together in papa's school ! How perfectly we understand each other !" Then she resumed her singing, to which I listened with wonder and admiration. In the evening I visited the Italian Opera, and, still under the influence of the enchantment I had experienced in the morning, I described in glowing terms the powers of the fair syren to several of my friends. " She is a perfect wonder," said I ; " her appearance will form an epoch in the musical world." " But," replied the person to whom I addressed these words, " no one has heard of her. If she were really so clever as you describe, surely her reputation must have travelled hither before her." I again expressed my high opinion of her talents, and the conviction that she would create a wonderful sensation. "I strongly suspect," said one of my friends, "that her Spanish origin tends not a little to enhance her merits in your eyes." "I confess that has some claim to my interest, but not so much as you imagine. I certainly feel proud to reflect that this beautiful and talented creature has Spanish blood in her veins; but that is all. A little time will, I think, show the justice of my anticipations."

A few days afterwards I assembled at my house a sort of musical jury—a party of unbelievers. They were, as I expected, struck with astonishment on seeing and hearing her. Maria Malibran was sublime as a dramatic singer, but her most triumphant efforts were those little extempore *fiorituri*, with which she was wont to electrify her hearers in small private circles. On these occasions, when she gave free scope to her own inspirations, she seemed like the very genius of music. What a fund of original ideas, what exquisite taste, did Madame Malibran evince, when she imparted new life to a composition, by adorning it, as it were, with the brilliant and vivid hues of the rainbow.

Before Madame Malibran had sung her first aria at my party, she had completely converted the little group of unbelievers into devout worshippers.

.

CHAPTER VIII.

Madame Malibran's *debút* at the Italian Opera in Paris—Her
apprehension of failure—Disadvantages she had to contend
against—Her triumphant success—Offers of engagements
—She concludes an engagement with the manager of the
Théâtre Italien—Her *debút* in Desdemona—Versatility of
her powers as a singer and actress—Remark of Crescentini
—Madame Malibran withdraws herself from her husband's
relations—She takes up her abode with Madame Naldi—
Authority exercised by that lady—The Cashmere shawl.

MADAME MALIBRAN made her first appearance
at the Grand Opera of Paris, in January
1828, in the part of Semiramide. The performance was for the benefit of Galli. For
the first time in her life she felt timidity.
She knew that on that night's performance her

future reputation depended. The part she had selected was not precisely fitted to her. The music did not fall on the best notes of her voice; and she had another obstacle to contend against in the size of the theatre, which was larger than any in which she had heretofore sung. These disadvantages were calculated to intimidate her; but nevertheless her natural courage enabled her to encounter them with spirit.

The first notes of her powerful voice which thrilled on the ears of the audience were followed by rapturous plaudits; all who witnessed her performance pronounced her to be a *prima donna* of the highest talent. She now received liberal offers for engagements. She at first hesitated between the Théâtre Italien and the Grand Opera; but she decided in favour of the former, and her choice was judicious. At the French opera, singing was at that time merely a sort of declamation, which would not have afforded free scope for the exercise of Madame

Malibran's peculiar talents. That style of singing, (in which the *cantabile* is nearly null,)
requiring vast power of lungs, would, in a very
few years, have exhausted the voice of Madame
Malibran, who, in the conscientious performance of her professional duties, thought only
of the present, and never considered the
future. She concluded an engagement with
the managers of the Théâtre Italien, and made
her *debût* in the part of Desdemona.

She speedily attained the most brilliant popularity. The Parisians were enthusiastic in
their admiration and applause : and Madame
Malibran, supported by the confidence which
success inspires, frequently reached sublimity
both in her singing and acting.

The vast compass of Madame Malibran's
voice, together with the versatility of her talent,
enabled her to perform in all Rossini's operas ;
and, in some instances, the two first parts in
the same opera ; for example, in Semiramide,
in which she could sustain, in equal perfection,

the character of Arsace and that of the Queen
of Babylon. Her personation of Desdemona
was a touching picture of sensibility and melancholy. Her Rosina was the perfection of playful grace and arch gaiety; whilst she drew
tears from the eyes of all who beheld her in
Ninetta, in the Gazza Ladra. It is impossible
to conceive a more perfect personification of
resigned sorrow, partaking of fatalism.

Crescentini, when asked his opinion of a
singer whose talent had been greatly and un-
justly extolled, replied, " *Canta bene, ma non
mi persuade.*" This observation could not have
been applied to Madame Malibran. On hearing that fascinating singer, it was impossible
not to identify oneself with her, because she
identified herself with her part. Her impassioned soul, by some irresistible power of
sympathy, communicated to others the sentiments which she so well experienced and
expressed. Talent alone, whatever be its
degree of superiority, is incapable of producing

this magical effect: true feeling is the secret
spell.   That which emanates from the heart
has alone the power to reach the hearts of
others.

Madame Malibran soon had reason to be
dissatisfied with the treatment she experienced
from her husband's relatives. She complained
of the irksome tutelage to which she was subjected, both in person and purse; but the
want of protection, and the fear of that censure
which her extreme youth and her independent
position might draw down upon her, induced
her to prolong for some time her residence with
her sister-in-law. However, one day, in a moment
of irritation, she sent for a coach, and, taking
with her her trunks, she drove off, unknown to
her relatives, and took up her abode with Madame Naldi.

Availing herself of that freedom of manners
which the theatrical profession admits of, she
might, with perfect propriety, have resided
alone; but she was young, and surrounded by

admirers, and in the *naïve* purity of her sentiments she felt the necessity of protection.
She therefore submitted voluntarily to the
authority of Madame Naldi, an old friend of
her family, and a woman of imperious and aus-
tere manners. It was truly touching to see her
yield to the advice, and submit to the little
sacrifices which her friend exacted from her.
To Madame Naldi she readily resigned that
self-will which, to all others, was so unbending;
and when, by any little fits of ill-humour or
irritability, she thought she had offended her
friend, she would load her with caresses, and ask
her pardon with the humility of a child. All
the letters which were addressed to Madame
Malibran, as well as all which she herself wrote,
were shown to Madame Naldi. That lady had
the use of her money, and allowed her only as
much as would provide her with the strictest
necessaries.

Shortly before her death, at the time when
her fortune was so brilliant, Madame Malibran

called the attention of a friend to an old Cashmere shawl which she wore; " I prefer wearing
this old shawl," she said, " to any other that I
have got.   It was the first Cashmere shawl I
ever possessed, and I experience a certain degree
of pleasure in calling to mind all the trouble it
cost me to prevail on Madame Naldi to allow
me to purchase it."

CHAPTER IX.

The performance of separate acts of different operas—First introduction of that custom—Madame Malibran's disapproval of it—Effects of the custom on a musical audience —Due preparation of the ear for musical enjoyment—Advantage of displacing the acts of an opera—Different impressions produced by musical compositions, according to the modifications of time and place—Contrary opinions sometimes pronounced on celebrated singers—Sensations produced by excessive delicacy of the musical ear.

ABOUT the time of Madame Malibran's appearance in Paris commenced the custom, now so prevalent, of performing separate acts of different operas.

Our prima donna felt a certain degree of repugnance in conforming with this incongruity, and she frequently told me that she experienced great difficulty in entering into the spirit of her part, when she had to commence at the second act. This may be readily conceived.

Such a mode of varying the amusements of the public, or rather of helping operatic managers out of their embarrassments, is certainly at variance with common sense. Nothing short of the indifference with which the Italians regard the meaning of an opera libretto could have given rise to the introduction of so absurd a practice.

But if this custom of dividing operas piece-meal be revolting to reason, it is not revolting to the ear of the amateur. The sense of hearing, like each of our other faculties, is endowed with a certain degree of power which has its first developement, its perfection, and decay.

However practised the ear may be in seizing the shades of harmony, it nevertheless requires a little preparation. The musical ear, on being roused from the apathy resulting from inaction,

experiences a certain degree of confusion, which
is dispelled only in proportion as the action of
the organ is restored by exercise. When that
action is fully restored, the enjoyment is complete; because the sense being completely developed is in the plenitude of its power. The
action of the organ at first communicates pleasure: after continued action weariness ensues;
and at length fatigue irritates, and renders it not
only incapable of enjoying, but even of judging.

Every one must have observed that the first
morceaux of an opera are never duly appreciated, unless they have been previously heard
as detached performances;—that the last pieces
of an opera are rarely listened to, unless the
drama be very short;—and that, in general,
the success of an opera is decided between the
end of the first act and the commencement of
the second.

It is, therefore, evident that in order to mul-
tiply the enjoyment we derive from music, it

would be desirable to hear all the best portions
of an opera at the moment when our faculties
are in the plenitude of their power for receiving
impressions; that is to say, not at the moment
when they were first roused into action, or when
wearied by exercise. Consequently, by displacing the acts of an opera, the different parts
are heard at the proper moment; that is to say,
when the musical ear is in the plenitude of its
power.

I have oftener than once amused myself in
deducing these ideas from my own impressions.
Experience has fully convinced me of the justice
of my observations.

This custom of performing separate acts of
operas confers the charm of novelty on many
old productions. I have often listened to
musical compositions which appeared to be
invested with additional freshness and beauty,
merely by the modifications produced on my
feelings by time and place!—How many con-
fused and fugitive recollections — how many

sensations of the mind may be conjured up by the electric strains of songs which we have once listened to carelessly, and perhaps unconsciously!

The place we occupy in a theatre—the particular tier in which our box may be situated— the manner in which the sound reaches the ear—all these circumstances have their influence on the sensations of persons who are keenly alive to the charms of music.

On quitting the Opera House, how frequently do we hear the most contrary comments on the performance! " Rubini did not sing well," says one; whilst another voice exclaims, " Rubini was divine this evening." " Grisi was in excellent voice," remarks one. " I thought she screamed horribly," says another. This diversity of opinions might perhaps be traced to the place which each interlocutor occupied in the theatre, and perhaps even to the degree of comfortable accommodation which his seat afforded.

It is certain that the sensibility of the musical
ear may become so irritable that a harsh voice,
or a false intonation, will cause the most annoy-
ing effects, even to the excitement of spasmodic
sensations.

CHAPTER X.

MADAME MALIBRAN'S popularity daily increased. The appearance of Mademoiselle Sontag * at the Théâtre Italien was a new sti-

* Now Countess Rossi.

mulus, which contributed, if possible, to improve her talents.

Whenever Sontag obtained a brilliant triumph, Malibran would weep, and exclaim, " Why does she sing so divinely?" The tears excited by these feelings of emulation were the harbingers of renewed exertion and increased improvement.

An earnest desire was felt by many distinguished amateurs to hear these two charming singers together in one opera. But they were mutually fearful of each other, and for some time they cautiously avoided being brought together.

One evening they met at a concert at my house. A little plot was formed against them, and about the middle of the concert it was proposed that they should sing the duo from Tancredi.

For some moments they evidently betrayed fear and hesitation; but at length they consented, and they advanced to the piano amidst the plaudits of the company.

They stood gazing at each other with a look of distrust and confusion; but at length the closing chord of the introduction roused their attention, and the duo commenced.

The applause was rapturous, and was equally divided between the charming singers. They themselves seemed delighted at the effect they had produced, and astonished to discover how groundless had been their mutual fear. They joined hands, and, inclining affectionately towards each other, they interchanged the kiss of friendship with all the ardour and sensibility of youth.

This moving scene will remain indelibly impressed on the memories of all who witnessed it.

Amidst the brilliant existence which she had now entered upon, Maria Malibran preserved all her natural childishness of manner and simplicity of taste.

She was totally ignorant of everything connected with domestic management and the expenditure of money.

She had been so wholly devoted to her professional studies and avocations, that she seemed to be, as it were, excluded from the circle of real life. She had no taste for luxury, and she never indulged in superfluous expenses; but her bounty was ever unsparingly bestowed on those who needed it. If a case of distress amongst her operatic colleagues reached her ears, she would immediately send a sum of money for the relief of the suffering party. But her aid was not confined to pecuniary donations· She would get up a concert for the benefit of the distressed person or family, use her influence to sell tickets, and break with the operatic manager, if he refused her permission to sing. In this manner her talents and her earnings were constantly devoted to purposes which reflect the highest honour on her generous nature.

Towards the close of one of the seasons of the Parisian opera, a young female, one of the chorus-singers, formed an engagement at the

Opera in London. According to the terms of her engagement, she was to commence her duty in London on a certain night; but she found herself unable to quit Paris, for want of money to pay her travelling expenses. As soon as these circumstances reached the ears of Madame Malibran, she immediately offered to sing at the concert which some persons were exerting themselves to get up for the benefit of the poor chorus-singer.

It may readily be conceived that the announcement of Madame Malibran's name in the bills was a powerful attraction; and accordingly the concert-room was crowded to excess.

At the hour fixed for the commencement of the concert Madame Malibran had not arrived, and the fear of a disappointment began to create uneasiness.

When the performances were nearly half over, Madame Malibran presented herself, and stepping up to the young chorus-singer, she said in a whisper, " I am rather late, my dear, but the audience shall lose nothing, for I will sing all the pieces set down for me. But, as I promised you my services for the whole evening, I intend to keep my word. I have been singing at a concert given by the Duke of Orleans, and his Royal Highness has presented me with three hundred francs. There, take the money, it is yours !"

Nothing gratified Madame Malibran more than to depart from her usual cast of character, the queens and heroines of the serious opera, and to take comic and even burlesque parts. Thus she voluntarily appeared in the second-rate character of Fidalma in the *Matrimonio Segreto*, and I once heard her say that she should like much to take the trivial character of the Duenna in the Barber of Seville, merely for the sake of wearing the comical dress.

There being very few parts of this class which she could with any degree of propriety appear in on the operatic stage, she amused herself by acting burlesque characters in private theatricals in her own house.

She possessed admirable talent for caricature. In this respect her humour was not inferior to that of Vernet or Madame Vautrin.

All musical amateurs, in the very highest circle of Parisian society, were eager to obtain invitations to Madame Malibran's private theatricals, and every one was delighted with her performance of the burlesque characters of comedy. But amidst the admiration with which she was greeted, both in public and private, she had the mortification to learn that she had been bitterly assailed in an English Journal, (Galignani's Messenger,) and that the attack had been copied into several French papers.

From the fear of being too much influenced either by praise or blame, Madame Malibran made it a rule never to read the criticisms on her performances which appeared in the public journals. She would, therefore, have remained in ignorance of the attack in Galignani's Mes-

senger, had not her attention been called to it
by a peculiar circumstance.

Baron de Fremont, who was a great admirer
of Madame Malibran's talent, happened to read
the article above alluded to, and was highly
indignant at its manifest injustice, though he
had not been present at the representation to
which it referred. It was natural to expect
that some one who had witnessed the performance so severely censured would step forward
and refute, by his own knowledge of facts, the
assertions of Madame Malibran's assailant.
But several days elapsed, and no champion
declared himself. Baron de Fremont called on
Madame Malibran, showed her the article, and
en vrai preux begged that she would permit
him to take up her defence, by addressing a
letter to the editor of Galignani's Messenger.
Madame Malibran was deeply sensible of this
act of kindness. It was the more serviceable to
her, inasmuch as the attack was calculated to
injure her in the opinion of the English public,

before whom she was engaged to appear a few months subsequently.

The following is a letter which Madame Malibran addressed to Baron de Fremont, returning thanks for the service he had rendered her.

Paris, —— 1829.

" Sir,

" I am deeply sensible of your kind exertions to serve me, and I feel unable to express the fulness of my gratitude. I have been so occupied in studying the part of Tancredi, that I have not been able to snatch a moment to reply to your two kind letters, and to tell you that I had requested one of our good friends to do what you recommended. I believe that everything is now done. It is true that I have expressed to Madame de Orfila my wish to be present at Madame Lebrun's masked ball; but I cannot take the liberty of soliciting an invita-

tion for my brother, as I have not the honour
of being acquainted with M. Lebrun. I therefore thank you for your good intentions, but
I do not wish that this ball should afford another
pretext for drawing down censure.

" I beg you will accept every assurance of the
grateful sentiments with which I remain, Sir,

" Your obliged

" M. MALIBRAN."

I must needs confess that I always experienced a certain degree of dissatisfaction when
I saw Maria Malibran assume the representation
of grotesque characters. I could not endure to
see her distort and disfigure that beautiful countenance, which was so well fitted to reflect the
noblest sentiments of the soul.

But this extraordinary woman, like all persons
of superior genius, was actuated by an uncontrollable desire to exercise all the various talents

with which she was so liberally gifted. She was not prompted by vanity, but by the force of her own genius.

CHAPTER XI.

MADAME MALIBRAN took her benefit on the 31st of March. The performance was Otello. Public enthusiasm was at its height.

On this occasion wreaths and bouquets of flowers were for the first time thrown on the stage of the Italian Opera at Paris.

Madame Malibran therefore received the first offerings of this delightful homage, so appropriate to female taste, and so well calculated to make an impression on the female heart.

Maria Malibran's nervous temperament and romantic turn of feeling inspired her with a passionate love of flowers. During her performance of Desdemona, on the evening of her benefit above alluded to, she betrayed her fondness for flowers in a singular way. When Desdemona lay dead on the stage, and the Moor in his frenzied grief was preparing to inflict upon himself the blow which was to lay him prostrate at her side, Madame Malibran, fearing the destruction of the bouquets and wreaths which lay scattered round her, exclaimed in a low tone of voice, " Take care of my flowers ! Do not crush my flowers !"

As a relaxation from the fatigues of her professional exertions, she set off, at the end of June, to pass a few weeks at the Château de

Brizay, the residence of the Countess de Sparre.* That amiable lady, whose talents entitle her to hold the first rank among musicians, as her virtues befit her to occupy the highest station in society, cherished a cordial and sincere friendship for Maria Malibran.

When in the country, our prima donna, forgetting the crown of Semiramide and the harp of Desdemona, used sometimes to sally forth on her rural rambles disguised in the garb of a young student. Dressed in a short blouse, a silk handkerchief tied negligently round her neck, and a light *casquette* on her head, she naturally found herself more safe and under less restraint than she could have been in female habiliments.

She would rise at six in the morning, and go out, sometimes taking a fowling-piece, to enjoy the sport of shooting. At other times she would go out on horseback, always selecting the most spirited horse she could find. After

* The daughter of Naldi, the celebrated buffo singer.

galloping over hill and dale, at the risk of
breaking her neck, fording rivers, and exposing
herself to every danger, she would return and
quell the apprehensions of her friends, who
were often painfully alarmed for her safety.
During the remainder of the day she would
amuse herself with all sorts of childish games
and exercises.

Among the visiters at the Château de Brizay,
was Dr. D——, an old friend of the Countess de
Sparre. The doctor was a remarkably kind-
hearted and charitable man, and the gravity of
his manners formed an amusing contrast to the
gaiety of Madame Malibran.

She one day took it into her head to disguise
herself as a peasant girl. Her costume was
perfect; the pointed cap with long *barbes*, the
gold cross, the shoe-buckles, — nothing was
wanting.

She coloured her skin so as to give the
semblance of a swarthy sunburnt complexion,
and stuffed out her cheeks with cotton, to

impart an appearance of plumpness to her face. Thus disguised, she one day presented herself to the doctor, and addressing him in the *patois* of the province, which she could mimic in perfection, told him a piteous tale of misfortune. Her mother was ill, and had broken her arm, &c. " I have heard, sir, that you are a very clever doctor, and I hope you will give me something to cure my poor mother. I assure you we are in miserable poverty !"

Dr. D. prescribed some remedies, gave her a little money, and Madame Malibran took her leave.

In the evening, when the doctor related to the company the visit he had received, Madame Malibran affected to listen with great interest to his story, and expressed regret that she had not seen the peasant girl.

The hoax was several times repeated, and at length the pretended peasant girl gave the old doctor to understand that she was deeply smitten with him. The doctor and the other

visiters at the château were highly amused at
this strange infatuation of the peasant girl.
Madame Malibran constantly expressed regret
that she could not get sight of the fair *inamo-
rata*, always accounting for her absence by a
headache, or a visit to some poor family in the
village.

One day, the pretended peasant, emboldened
by the success of her hoax, took the doctor's
arm, and walked round the garden in conversation with him. The poor doctor did not attempt to withdraw his arm. He quietly resigned
himself to his fate; but turning to the persons
who accompanied him, he said, " What a flattering conquest I have made !"

No sooner had he uttered these words, than
a smart *soufflet* convinced him of the propriety
of being gallant, even to a peasant girl.

" And when did you ever make a better, you
ungrateful man ?" exclaimed Madame Malibran
in her natural tone of voice, which she had
hitherto disguised by means of the stuffing she
had put into her mouth.

Poor Dr. D. stood bewildered with astonishment, whilst all present joined in a roar of laughter, at the same time complimenting Madame Malibran on the perfection of her disguise.

But these playful sallies did not divert Madame Malibran's thoughts from the exercise of that generosity which was inherent in her nature. Some days after the scene above described, she observed that Dr. D. appeared low-spirited and abstracted. She questioned him on the subject of his unusual dulness, but could gain no satisfactory answer. She soon, however, learned that a sister of the doctor, who had suffered several sad reverses of fortune, now found herself completely ruined by a fire, which had destroyed her house, and with it all the property she possessed.

This disaster not only obliged Dr. D. to transmit pecuniary aid to his sister, but also to make a journey into the south of France, to assist her by his advice. As his own fortune was very limited, he found it no easy task to accomplish these duties.

Madame Malibran immediately despatched letters, directing that the house should be rebuilt at her expense.

This act of generous bounty was executed with such promptitude and secrecy, that, just at the moment when Dr. D. was about to start on his journey to the south, he received a letter from the mayor of the village in which his sister resided. This letter acknowledged the receipt of the sum *sent by him,* assuring him that it should be applied according to his directions, &c. The fact was, that Madame Malibran had sent the requisite instructions to the mayor for rebuilding the house; and she had so fully anticipated every want of the suffering family, as to render Dr. D.'s journey unnecessary.

During the life of Madame Malibran, neither Dr. D. nor his sister knew who was their benefactor; but, after her decease, some me-

moranda found among her papers disclosed the
secret.   A stone is now fixed on the front of the
house, bearing the following inscription :

REBATIE

PAR LES POINS BIENFAISANTS

DE MADAME MALIBRAN.

This act of generosity is the more worthy of
admiration, inasmuch as, at the time of its performance, Madame Malibran had scarcely commenced her theatrical career, and a great
portion of the emoluments arising from her
exertions was despatched to her husband in
America.

CHAPTER XII.

Madame Malibran returns to Paris—Terms of her engagement at the Théâtre Italien—The operatic company—Madame Malibran's appearance in *Matilda di Sabrano*, the *Gazza Ladra*, and the *Cenerentola*—The prison duet in the *Gazza Ladra*—Halevy's opera of Clary—Madame Malibran's impressive performance of the character of the heroine—She sets off for London, accompanied by Madame Naldi—Her engagement at the King's Theatre—Her terms for singing at private parties—Charitable act—Madame Malibran engaged to sing at Bath and Bristol—She proceeds to Brussels.

AFTER a visit of three months at the Château de Brizay, Madame Malibran returned to Paris, where the operatic season was about to commence.

She concluded an engagement with M. Laurent, the manager of the Théâtre Italien, on the same terms as those of the preceding year;

viz. eight hundred francs for each night of performance, and a free benefit.

The principal members of the operatic company
were—Madame Malibran, Mademoiselle Sontag,
Donzelli, Zuccheli, and Graziani.   Madame
Malibran appeared in Otello, and was greeted
with all the enthusiasm which her performances
of the preceding season had elicited.

On the 13th of October she appeared in the
new character of Matilda di Sabrano. She
sang and acted with her usual excellence ; but
the music of the part being better adapted to
the high and flexible tones of a soprano voice,
was therefore better suited to the powers
of Mademoiselle Sontag, to whom Madame
Malibran shortly after surrendered the part.

In the Cenerentola, and the Gazza Ladra,
Madame Malibran appeared with prodigious
success. She was charming in the homely costume of Cenerentola, and she acted the part
with the most captivating simplicity and *naïveté*.

The victim-like resignation which she maintained in the presence of her father, suddenly changed when she was left alone with her sisters. She then assumed a haughty and pouting manner, which imparted an air of novelty to the character.

The splendid finale, " Non piu mesta," was admirably adapted to Malibran's powers, as was likewise the *cantabile* in the finale to the first act. The vast extent of notes embraced in these two compositions enabled Madame Malibran to display the full resources of her voice and style, and she astonished all who heard her by the original and happy flights of her fancy.

Madame Malibran was the first singer who revealed the beauty of the prison duo in the opera of the Gazza Ladra. Previously to her performance of Ninetta, that composition had been listened to with indifference, and indeed it had been often entirely omitted, as though it were a production of inferior merit.

How unfortunate it would be for musical

composers, if they did not sometimes find
singers capable of understanding and imparting
a due expression to their conceptions!

The duo above mentioned, which had been
neglected because it was not understood, obtained the greatest popularity after it had been
sung by Madame Malibran. She gave the
andante with an expression of prophetic and
touching melancholy, and then dashed boldly
into the allegro, defying, as it were, the power
of fate. Her rapid transitions from the lower
to the upper tones of her voice excited at once
wonder and delight.

The whole history of poor Ninetta appeared
to be summed up in this duo, when sung with
the powerful expression which Madame Malibran imparted to it. The life of girlish inno
cence and joy chequered by gloomy forebod-
ings, the torments of unjust persecution, the
fury of despair, the resignation of innocence—
all were admirably and vividly portrayed.

I never witnessed the performance of the

drama here alluded to—not even in the operatic form, in which the music tends to soften down its vivid colouring—without being forcibly impressed with the natural truth of the subject, and the example it affords of human injustice.

On the 9th of December Madame Malibran appeared in the opera of Clary, which M. Halevy composed expressly for her. The performance was crowned with brilliant success. The opera contained a great deal of beautiful music.

Nothing could be finer than Madame Malibran's acting in the scene in which Clary first appears, magnificently dressed, and surrounded by all the allurements which love and wealth can bestow. When she expressed her remorse and regret, and when memory reverted to the days of her childhood and her father's cottage, tears of penitence seemed to roll down her cheeks.

In this scene the thrilling tones of Malibran's voice vibrated through the hearts of her auditors. The impressive effect of her performance

will never be erased from the memory of those
who witnessed it.

Then, again, how admirably she acted the
scene in which she discovered her lover's trea-
chery, when he frankly avows that he never had
the intention of making her his wife! What
noble pride was expressed in her accents! how
truly dignified she seemed, even in the depths
of her wretchedness!

Maria Malibran affords one of the few examples of the capability of producing ineffaceable
impressions in an art whose effects are in their
very nature fugitive. She was one of the gifted
few whom Nature endows with the union of
those rare qualities which serve to reveal all the
power of the histrionic art.

All who have seen Madame Malibran in the
character of Clary must have been struck with
her exquisite acting in the scene in which,
having resumed the humble garb of a village
girl, she prepares to depart, renouncing her
fatal illusions and vain hopes. She opens the

window to effect her escape : a ray of moonlight falls full on the portrait of her lover, and
she pauses to gaze on it. It would be vain to
attempt to describe the admirable expression of
her countenance and attitude, or the thrilling
accents of her voice, whilst she took a last farewell of the picture.

It is to be regretted that the opera of Clary
has not been more frequently performed ;
though, after Malibran, it would have been
difficult for any other to undertake the part.
The opera was highly creditable to the talent of
its composer.

On the 2nd of April, 1829, after the close of
the Théâtre Italien, Madame Malibran left
Paris for London, accompanied by Madame
Naldi. She was engaged by Laporte to sing
at the King's Theatre, the terms of her engagement being seventy-five guineas per night, and
a benefit. In London she was greeted with the
echo of the applause she had so deservedly
earned in Paris. She performed in Otello,

Semiramide, the Gazza Ladra, the Capuleti,
and the Cenerentola.

But the happiness of thus finding herself the
object of public admiration was not without
its antidote. She experienced some little annoyances in her intercourse with private society.
It was thought, I know not why, that her demand of twenty-five guineas for singing at a
private party was exorbitant. That sum had,
however, been readily granted to Pasta; and
as Madame Malibran considered that it would
be doing herself injustice to lower her demand, a little unpleasantness of feeling ensued, and she sang but seldom in private
circles.

This sort of exile annoyed her, not from any
considerations of pecuniary interest, but because
she attached great importance to the advantage
of mingling in the higher circles of society.
Nevertheless, she was received with the most
gratifying cordiality in the houses of several
members of the English aristocracy; and in

London, as in Paris, she formed many real friends in the most exalted rank of life.

On the eve of Madame Malibran's departure from London, she performed an act of charity which well deserves to be recorded. On her return home from the opera, her ears still ringing with the plaudits which her performance had elicited, she beheld, on alighting from her carriage, a poor woman, with two little children, sitting on the steps of the door, and imploring charity.

The night was cold and rainy. Madame Malibran instantly ordered that the poor woman and her children should be admitted to the house, and that they should be warmed and fed. She collected some articles of clothing for the children, and putting five guineas into the hand of the mother, she said, " Take this, my good woman, and pray for me."

Madame Malibran was engaged to sing in eight concerts at Bath and Bristol, for the sum of seventy guineas each performance. These

concerts were not, however, to commence until
the end of September, or the beginning of October; and Madame Malibran accordingly
availed herself of the respite thus afforded her
to pay a visit to Brussels, where she was impatiently expected.   In that city she sang at
several concerts, and was received with increased
favour.

CHAPTER XIII.

HERETOFORE Madame Malibran's whole soul had been absorbed by the love of her art, and to excel in it appeared to be the sole object of her thoughts and wishes. Her character was pure, and her conduct had been marked by the most scrupulous propriety. But, at the period to which I am now about to advert, her heart became susceptible to that passion which, in a nature like hers, could not fail to determine the fate of her after life.

The object of her attachment was a young artist, whose talents, even then, entitled him to rank among the first musicians of the day. Maria Malibran's choice was therefore perfectly congenial with her position as well as with her taste; and, amidst the seductions to which she was exposed, that choice proves the pure and elevated feelings by which her inclinations were guided.

One day a friend was rallying her on the ardent passion with which she had inspired one of her admirers. " Why, I confess," she replied, with an air of simple earnestness, " that I do believe he loves me, but what of that? I do not love him. I do not wish to set myself up as a heroine of virtue. I know the dangers

to which I am exposed. I am young, untram-
melled by pecuniary dependence, married to a
man old enough to be my grandfather; my
husband two thousand leagues apart from me,
and I exposed to every temptation—the probability is, that I shall fall in love some day or
another. But rest assured that whenever I
do, I will not play the coquette. When I meet
with the man capable of winning my heart, I
will honestly tell him that I love him, and my
affection will never change.

She kept her word.

M. de Beriot, the distinguished violinist, had
left Belgium, his native country, to pass the
winter in Paris. During that season Madame
Malibran and De Beriot met several times at
concerts and musical parties, and their united
talents were the theme of admiration.

Madame Malibran, though she knew but
little of the young violinist, felt a deep interest
for him. This interest was excited not merely
by his talent, which she admired with all the

enthusiasm natural to her ardent feeling; but she knew that he was unfortunate, and that was a powerful claim on her sympathy

De Beriot had conceived an attachment for Mademoiselle S——, but his passion was not returned, the lady's affections being engaged to the individual who afterwards became her husband.

Pity is nearly allied to love in the heart of a woman of ardent and romantic feeling; and whilst Madame Malibran pitied De Beriot, she loved him without being conscious of it. They separated at the close of the spring, but they met again at Brussels.

One evening they were at the Château de Chimay, De Beriot played a concerto which enchanted all who heard him. At its conclusion Madame Malibran stepped up to him, and taking his hand in hers, in a faltering voice expressed her admiration of his performance. Her eyes were overflowing with tears, and she was agitated by the most powerful emotions. Whilst endeavouring to disguise her embarrass-

ment, by giving utterance to a string of com-
pliments and congratulations, some words escaped her which sufficiently denoted her real
sentiments.

From that moment the hearts of these two
young artists were linked together in the purest
mutual affection.

Madame Malibran returned to England to
fulfil her professional engagements.

She soon began to feel annoyed by the
restraint imposed on her by Madame Naldi,
and she no longer made that lady the confidante
of her correspondence.

Madame Naldi suspected Madame Malibran's
attachment for De Beriot, and she decidedly
disapproved it. Maria listened to her remonstrance and advice with apparent deference, but
she was in reality deeply mortified, and from
that moment she resolved to take the first
opportunity of emancipating herself from a
restraint to which but a short time previously
she voluntarily subjected herself.

Madame Malibran landed at Calais on the
26th of October, and reached Paris on the
28th. She took up her residence in a small
house, which, through the medium of a friend,
she had engaged in the Rue de Provence.
Although her circumstances and position were
unchanged, yet she seemed at this time to
attach particular importance to the fact of
residing in a house of her own. It is possible
that vague thoughts, which perhaps she dared
not avow even to herself, rendered her sensible
to the value of entire independence.

The season of the Italian Opera commenced
in Paris with more than usual brilliancy. To
the united talents of Mesdames Malibran and
Sontag were added those of Madame Pizzaroni.
It is impossible to conceive the effect produced
by the combined performances of these three
extraordinary singers.

The success of Madame Pizzaroni, in spite
of the unfavourable impression produced by her
personal appearance, reflects equal honour on

her talents and the good sense of the public.
The merit of her singing gained the suffrage
even of those who had at first been prejudiced
by her total deficiency of beauty. Her singing
may be ranked among the greatest triumphs of
the vocal air.

Her contralto voice, though possessing great
compass, was very unequal in its quality. In
singing upon some of her middle notes, she
was unfortunately obliged to twist her mouth
in such a manner that the tone thus produced
had a very peculiar and strange effect.

Notwithstanding the general purity and beauty
of Pizzaroni's style, some connoisseurs are of
opinion that the peculiar twist of the mouth
above mentioned was merely the result of an
unfortunate habit. But I doubt this. It always
appeared to me that the distortion was an un-
avoidable necessity, and that the notes in
question could not have been sung without it.

The best singers have two different me-
thods of forming their tones: first, by a strict

adherence to the rules of art; and secondly, by modifying those rules according to the peculiar nature of the voice. Art will enable a singer to turn even natural imperfections to advantage;* and there are defects of voice which can be modified only by deviating from the rules of art. There are many examples of great singers who, after strictly adhering for a series of years to the principles. of art, contract a faulty and at length a bad style ; because, their voices having changed, they are obliged to sing as *they can,* and not as *they would.*

Maria Malibran made her re-appearance at

---

* That depth of expression which is one of the principal charms of Madame Pasta's singing, is in a great degree due to the irregularity of the tones of her voice. Her lower tones, which are somewhat harsh and husky, are admirably fitted for the expression of vehement passion, and are the more effective owing to the beautiful and unexpected contrast presented by the sweetness of the upper tones. We are frequently impressed with a profound sensation of melancholy by the sort of guttural tone produced by some singers in the sudden transition from the *voce di petto* to the *voce di testa.*

the Théâtre Italien in her favourite character of Desdemona. Otello was speedily followed by Tancredi, and by Zingarelli's Romeo and Giulietta.

In the two last-mentioned operas Madame Malibran was powerfully seconded by the talents of the charming Mademoiselle Sontag, who performed the character of Amenaide in Tancredi, and that of Giulietta in Zingarelli's opera.

Madame Malibran had now become the idol of all frequenters of the opera. With her admirable singing she combined the talent of a great tragedian. Her acting was never studied—it was the result of her own inspirations; and if the ardour of those inspirations occasionally carried her beyond the limits of the circle prescribed by conventional custom, it cannot be denied that she often reached the sublime.

She never took lessons either in action or declamation. She was the pupil of nature;

and being endowed with an exquisite perception of the natural and the beautiful, she could,
without the aid of art, produce the most powerful effects. Her acting always came home to
the hearts of her auditors.

Professional advantage, seconded by the dictates of a more powerful interest, induced De
Beriot to revisit Paris. Madame Malibran was
overjoyed to see him. She received him with
tenderness mixed with reserve, for she stood
in great fear of public opinion. She already
felt grievously annoyed by the conviction, that
if she was received in society, it was only on
account of her talent.

Being naturally proud, and feeling a proper
consciousness of her own merit, she was painfully mortified to observe that, in reference to
herself, a line of demarcation was drawn between
rank and talent—between the equality imposed
by friendship, and the mere interest accorded
by patronage. How often would a cold look

or a haughty gesture inflict a deep wound on her sensitive heart, and rouse her from her dream of triumph!

Her life was made up of a series of contrasts. On the one hand she beheld a throng of admirers, who, enchanted by her powerful talent, offered to her the incense of adoration. But that brow which could so nobly bear a crown, shrank blushingly beneath the cold aristocratic salute. On returning home from a party, she has been known to burst into tears, exclaiming, " I am merely the opera singer—nothing more —the slave whom they pay to minister to their pleasure !"

From this it might naturally be presumed that Malibran would have felt gratified when a lady of high rank invited her to a party, and from motives of delicacy cautiously refrained from requesting her to sing. But no such thing! Such was her strange eccentricity of character, that though overwhelmed with attentions, she returned home ill-humoured and

dissatisfied, and satirically expressed her acknow-
ledgments for the generous and disinterested
politeness of which she had been the object.   It
was easy to perceive that, of all mortifications,
that which she most dreaded was to be deprived
of her crown of professional glory.

CHAPTER XIV.

Proposed trip to St. Petersburgh—Madame Malibran's dis
approval of the scheme—Coldness between her and De
Beriot—Elegant present sent by De Beriot to Madame
Malibran—She learns to play the harp—Her extraordinary
power of memory—Facility of learning her parts—Her capability of singing at sight—Chevalier Neukomm's mass—The
language of signs—The deaf and dumb youth—Madame
Malibran's conversation with him—Her riding and dancing
—Singers usually indifferent dancers.

DE BERIOT returned to Paris, attracted partly
by professional motives, but still more by the
presence of her whose affections he possessed.
Malibran, however, who was fully conscious of
the value of a reputation in a public character,
carefully concealed their *liaison*. One day De

Beriot informed her that he had made a most brilliant engagement to perform in Russia, and begged of her to accompany him, representing the advantage that would accrue from the union of their talents. But Madame Malibran's delicacy took the alarm. She rejected the proposition, pointing out how much her reputation would be compromised by such a step, and she reproached De Beriot for not having been himself the first to take that point into consideration. Some high words ensued between them, and for several days they met as strangers.

This state of things, however, did not last long; an explanation took place, and they became better friends than ever. Madame Malibran expressed a desire to learn the harp, and on the following morning De Beriot sent her a splendid one.

Touched by this mark of his attention, she studied the instrument, and in a very short time was enabled to accompany herself in

Desdemona's romance. She was afterwards induced to give it up, mainly through fear that it might injure her voice.

Madame Malibran had a most extraordinary power of memory. I have known her study an opera in the morning, and play in it the same evening. She had only to try over the music once, and she knew it perfectly.

One day when we were visiting Chevalier Neukomm, Maria took up a mass of his composition which was lying on the table. She sang it throughout, and accompanied herself without making a single mistake, although it was in manuscript and exceedingly difficult.

I saw her in the space of half an hour learn the language of signs—that is to say, the mode by which deaf and dumb persons communicate.

One day a friend called upon her, accompanied by a deaf and dumb youth. Madame Malibran was not aware of his infirmity, but the melancholy expression of his countenance

excited her interest. Her friend acquainted
her with the cause. She had never before seen
a deaf and dumb person, and she had no idea of
the language of signs.

She was deeply moved by the condition of
the poor lad, and with tears in her eyes she
drew her chair near to him. She endeavoured
to express herself to him by signs. He answered her in the same manner. She observed
and endeavoured to imitate him, and succeeded
so well that at the expiration of half an hour
she understood all the rules of the language,
and could carry on a fluent conversation in it.

Madame Malibran was fond of all active
exercises. She was an excellent horsewoman,
but an indifferent dancer. Singers in general
evince but little talent for dancing, and, what is
still more singular, they frequently keep very
bad time. Another curious fact is, that musicians are rarely sensible to the charms of
poetry.

How are these anomalies to be accounted

for? The idea that naturally suggests itself is, that the vast developement of one sense absorbs the power of the rest. But if it be true that dancing and music, as well as music and poetry, are like plants of one family, and may flourish on the same stem, it is not very easy to account for the extraordinary phenomenon.

CHAPTER XV.

M. Malibran arrives from America—His base deception previous to his marriage—He agrees to live apart from his wife—Madame Malibran's wish to obtain a divorce—She writes to General Lafayette—The General's last love—Madame Malibran's taste for charades and riddles—M. Viardot—An anecdote—Madame Malibran's musical compositions.

MEANWHILE M. Malibran came unexpectedly from America. His wife, who had hitherto aided him by her exertions, heard of his arrival with dismay. It was quite impossible she could respect him; the manner in which all his promises, both to herself and her father, had been broken, banished any esteem she might perhaps have felt for him.

He had agreed to give 100,000 francs
(£4,000) to Garcia, as a compensation for the
loss of his daughter's services : he had pledged
himself instantly to withdraw his wife from a
fatiguing and irksome profession, and to secure
to her a respectable independence for life. Neither of these promises was fulfilled, nor could
he have ever intended to fulfil them, for when
he made them, he must have been conscious
he was on the eve of immediate bankruptcy.

The breach of the first pledge caused Maria's
friends to abandon her. The violation of the
second promise compelled her not only to
return to her profession for her own main-
tenance, but also for that of her husband, who,
foreseeing the coming storm, had by a base deception secured himself against want.

This man's arrival in Europe was the first
serious shock Maria Malibran suffered; she
saw at a glance the horror of her early
marriage. M. Malibran had now come to assert
his rights, and to share the fruit of his wife's

exertions. The form which appeared as a sha-
dow on the other side of the Atlantic became sub-
stance, and the pensioner suddenly announced
his arrival in the character of her lord and
master. However, by the mediation of mutual
friends, and the payment of a considerable sum,
he consented to live apart from her. But she
naturally felt that he might, whenever he
pleased, violate this agreement; a moment's
change of humour, a sudden thought, and he
possessed the legal right to insist on sharing
her home. This dreaded doom kept her in a
state of continual agitation.

One night, while lying on her sleepless couch,
a sudden thought struck her. In the morning
she communicated it to a legal gentleman of
considerable talent; but the marriage having
been celebrated in New York, it was necessary
to write for information to America, and
no further steps could be taken for several
months.

In the expectation that legal proceedings

would be instituted in America, Madame Malibran wrote to Lafayette, requesting him to use his interest in her behalf, and lend his powerful aid in assisting her. This she need scarcely have asked, since the veteran patriot regarded her with the affection of a father, bestowing on her that admiration which he was ever ready to accord to talent. Often would he laughingly say, " Maria Garcia is my last love; I don't think any one will supplant her."

Madame Malibran, about this time, made the acquaintance, or, perhaps I should more properly say, gained the friendship, of M. Viardot in rather an extraordinary manner. As that friendship formed a feature in her after life, I may relate the anecdote here. Madame Malibran was remarkably fond of riddles and charades, and delighted in puzzling people to guess them. One evening she was repeating a number of ingenious riddles at a soirée given by M. ——. All were laughing, guessing, and applauding her to the skies, when she perceived

M. Viardot quietly seated in a corner of the room, apparently taking no interest in that which amused the rest of the company. This piqued her. It is true, M. Viardot was almost a stranger; but then, again, no pretty woman likes to be neglected, even by one out of a thousand. Maria again uttered another sally of wit, but in vain she looked for a smile from the sedate gentleman in the corner. Determined no longer to bear this, she rose after her next charade, and approaching him, asked in a low voice, " Give me your opinion of my last."

" It was not good," gravely replied M. Viardot, " because——;" and here he entered into his reasons for condemning it.

She listened to him attentively, and when he had done speaking, she could not help remarking on the singularity of his disapproval, since every one else applauded her.

" True," rejoined Viardot, " they seek to please you by flattery. But I really esteem you; therefore prefer telling you the truth, even at the risk of displeasing you."

For an instant she looked attentively at him; then holding out her hand, she grasped his, saying, "At length I have found sincerity. Grant me your friendship—mine is yours for life."

I cannot refrain from relating another circumstance which occurred on the same evening. Madame Malibran, as I believe every one is aware, had a remarkable talent for musical composition. This talent, however, she exercised only for amusement, giving to her friends, or to charities, the pieces she composed. On this occasion Madame de —— was present: a lady for whom our fair cantatrice had the greatest respect, but whose pecuniary circumstances were deplorably reduced. Willingly would Maria Malibran have assisted her, but the pride of Madame —— precluded the possibility of a pecuniary offer; she, therefore, resorted to an ingenious little artifice to effect her generous purpose. Madame ——'s son, a lad of sixteen, was present.

" I understand that this young gentleman has a great talent for poetry," said Madame Malibran to the mother. " I am going to propose a little speculation between us. Having written six airs for publication, I want words for them: will you undertake to furnish them, and we will divide the profits ?"

The proposal was instantly accepted; the young poet produced the verses, and they were sent to Madame Malibran. The songs were never published; but Madame de —— received six hundred francs as her son's share of the profit arising from them.

In the month of February De Beriot started for Brussels, from whence, a few weeks afterwards, he wrote to Madame Malibran, through his sister, offering her a most advantageous engagement in Holland. Her pride again took the alarm, and for the second time this extraordinary pair quarrelled.

CHAPTER XVI.

THE London season again brought Maria back to England.

Several of her friends advised her to relinquish her London engagement; and it already began to be whispered that Laporte was in an

insolvent state.   But the chance of terms such
as she had before obtained was too tempting to
be rejected ; so, at all hazards, she determined
to keep her engagement.   On her arrival she
found that Madame Lalande was the prima
donna whom she herself was to succeed.   This
lady had become a considerable favourite in
England, which annoyed Madame Malibran not
a little.   Jealousy is a feeling which, in. a
greater or a lesser degree, pervades public
performers; nor do I believe any actor or
actress is capable of fairly judging of the merits
of another.   Notwithstanding her naturally
good disposition, Madame Malibran could never
endure a rival; but her feelings on this subject
are best described in her own language, contained in a letter addressed by her at this period
to an intimate friend.

" MY DEAREST AND BEST FRIEND,
" I determined not to trouble you till I should
have something worth writing about, but I

cannot now help breaking the ice. Though I have no particular subject to treat on, yet I feel sure you will be delighted to see my scribble ; for I judge from myself, and I know I should be delighted to see yours. I fancy I see you reading these lines, and striking your forehead, whilst you exclaim, ' What strange creatures women are !' They are indeed—I confess it. What can I say more ?

" Let me see if I can think of some little bit of news—I have it : I will give you an account of the *debút* of Madame Lalande.

" I went to the opera with Lady Flint, her husband, and her daughter ; and having taken my seat and adjusted my *lorgnette*, I impatiently awaited the entrance of the Pirato, who was to be represented by Donzelli.

" The overture commenced. Humph ! very so so. It is not effective. The curtain rose. The opening scene was pretty, and was loudly applauded. Dramatic authors and composers know how much they owe to the scene-painter.

" Enter Il Pirato. He blustered, and strutted about, sang loudly, enchanted the audience, and was clapped. In acknowledgment of the applause, Donzelli bowed at least thirty times, and continued bowing until he was actually behind the side-scenes.

" The first air was tolerable.

" Change of scene.

" Venga la bella Italiana,* said I to my little self. I was all impatience, and as she appeared I stretched over the box to catch a glimpse of her. Alas ! what a disappointment ! Picture to yourself a woman of about forty, with light hair and a vulgar broad face, with an unfavourable expression, a bad figure, as clumsy a foot as my own, and most unbecomingly dressed.

" The recitative commenced. Her voice trembled so, that none could find out whether it was sweet or harsh. I therefore waited patiently

---

* This is meant as a little bit of malice ; the fact being, that Madame Lalande was neither handsome nor an Italian.

for the cavatina.   It commenced, and the
prima donna opened her mouth with a long
tremulous note.

" Concluding that this arose from timidity,
I could not help pitying her. But, alas! the
undulating tones of her voice continued throughout, and utterly spoiled the pretty cavatina.
At its conclusion she was vociferously applauded, and made a thousand curtsies, which
is the custom in London. Next came the beautiful duet. In this she was just as cold and
tremulous as before. In a word, not to weary
you with a long account of each morçeau, she
finished her part in the same bad style in
which she began it.

" She had to sing a very fine air just before
the conclusion, where her husband and her
lover had been killed. She advanced to the
front of the stage, leading in her hand a little
child, who would very much have preferred going
to sleep to being thus dragged on the stage to
hear a lachrymose chant. Madame Lalande

sang it without spirit, and consequently produced no effect.   Notwithstanding this, she
was called for after the fall of the curtain, and
received great applause.   Yet the general
opinion is, that she was very mediocre.   ' *Or
vien il meglio,*' as Susanne says: I have discovered that this tremulous style is Madame
Lalande's constant manner of singing.   It is
her fashion—immovable, fixed, eternal !   You
may therefore guess how well our voices are
likely to blend together—two and two, like
three goats.   Her middle notes are wiry, and
have a harsh and shrill effect.   The opera con-
tains some good music, but it is decidedly
feeble.   There is a splendid trio sung by the
lover, the husband, and the wife.   The latter is
so constant and faithful to the Pirate, that when
the lover and the husband throw themselves together at her feet, she sternly refuses to follow
her consort.   Another person would, perhaps,
have described this scene more intelligibly,
which, by-the-bye, is very much like that

between Otello, Iago, and Desdemona.   But I, who know to whom I am writing, feel convinced you will understand me.   I shall therefore take no pains to clear up the mystery which always pervades my explanations.*

" The proverb says truly, ' Amongst wolves one learns to howl.' I perceive I can neither utter a single sentence, nor write a single line, without introducing some parenthesis.   How pleasant it is, when really interested in a subject, to have to wade zig-zag through a thou-

---

* Madame Malibran, in her letters, frequently expressed herself with so much vagueness, that it is not always easy to understand her allusions. There often appears to be a private understanding between herself and the person she addresses, which renders the correspondence unintelligible to those who do not possess the key to the subject referred to. Some of her letters appear nonsensical and mysterious to the un-initiated reader. I have, however, transcribed them word for word, considering such to be my duty as a faithful biographer, and believing the reader would rather peruse the genuine effusions of her eccentric mind than any garbled explanations, which after all might be erroneous.

sand interruptions before you arrive at the point you wish to come to. You understand what I mean. It is a hint I give you *en passant*, and one which I trust you will attend to when you write me those letters I so anxiously look for, telling me all about your health, your plans," &c.

I may here transcribe a few letters from Madame Malibran, written about the same period as the above.

" 29th April, 1830.

" I am to appear immediately, because Laporte is rather in a difficult position just now. He is losing nightly. Madame Lalande has done him harm, and he expects me to come and drag him out of his trouble.

" You know that the chimney-sweepers dance about the streets of London on the first of May, dressed out in tinsel and flowers, with their cheeks bedaubed with paint. Luckily I do not make my *debût* on that day. Comparisons might be drawn; but no doubt I shall have to endure comparisons no less complimentary.

" My fears have such an effect upon me, that I am downright ill; but enough of this subject.

" I am going to breakfast. To-night, after the opera, I'll again write, and tell you my fate."

" 30th April, 1830.

" I made my first appearance last night in the Cenerentola. My *debût* was what is called here a most successful one, though, if I had had the same reception in Paris, I should have reckoned it half a failure. However, I was called for at the conclusion of the opera, and was applauded from the boxes as well as the pit.

" My voice is said to have improved since last year, as well as my figure, which is much admired. Don't imagine that I am vain of that, but I am determined to tell you all. I am also considered very gracious for consenting to make my first appearance on Thursday, an evening generally considered unfashionable. But, as my name drew a full audience, I was well pleased, since it secures me in favour for the rest of the season. I saw, when I was on the stage, my friend *Louchard*; I nodded to him in such a way as to show that I did not wish to take any further notice of him. To-morrow I repeat the same character, and I have no doubt I shall do it better. This evening I sing at a concert for the benefit of ' decayed musicians.'

" Need I again assure you that you are everything to me? You know it well. To you I owe my present happiness, as well as that which I enjoyed in Paris. I still wear the ring you gave me—perfect emblem of our friendship—a knot which, the more you try to undo it, becomes the tighter. Is it not a perfect image of true affection, of pure and long-enduring friendship? Yes! the more I think on it, the more certain do I feel that friendship is eternal, enduring through ages to come, consoling us even after death. This reflection makes me long for eternity, and yet I feel there are also miseries which will live for ever.

" I have written to Viardot, and he has done all he could to comfort me in my distress. I have also told my unhappy story to Lady Flint;* she has mentioned it to one of her friends, who informs her he was himself extricated from a similar misfortune by an old nobleman, (above seventy years of age,) who knows the laws of almost every country by heart. This morning Sir George Warrender, who is the *old friend* of the still *older nobleman*, is coming to see me at twelve to talk it over. As I hazard nothing in doing so, I shall let him know as much as may suit my views, (*and not one word more*,) in order to get his advice upon the subject, and thus relieve my oppressed heart.

* She here evidently alludes to her divorce.

" If you were near me, and I could talk to you, I should seek no other consolation. But, my friend, I beseech you do not suddenly surprise me; when the happy day for our meeting is fixed, let me know it. Give me a little time to prepare for the happy event, and by anticipation enjoy my coming happiness. Yes, you are the source of my every delight; you alone can make the drooping plant once more raise its head. There is one flower, heart's-ease, which must be ever with you, because you are all goodness —because you delight in consoling the afflicted —because you counsel as a father—like a brother—because—because—but stay—I should never have done with my *becauses*, were I to enumerate all your merits.

" Adieu—I must go and dress to receive *the old friend of the old friend*, and after that I must attend rehearsal.

" Adieu—father, mother, brother, and sister— adieu!—for to me you are all these."

"May 1st.

"I have had company with me all day, which has prevented my writing. Even at this moment my carriage is waiting to take me to rehearsal; and if I keep it waiting, I shall be in the predicament of poor Cinderella : my coachman will turn into a rat, and my horses into a pair of mice. I will write you the result of this evening's performance—a fashionable evening here."

"May 1st.

"I have played, my dear friend, and can safely say a better house never was seen—full to suffocation; indeed many could not gain admittance. I sang better than on Thursday. The other performers were delighted with me. They declare they like me very much, and they came after the opera to congratulate me. I heard them, as they went away, say to each other, ' This is something like singing—what splendid talent !' This is very gratifying to

me, though I know it must give pain to others;
but I can't help that."

The foregoing letter depicts Malibran in her
true character. It exhibits that mixture of the
frivolous and the serious which characterised
her manners and conversation. Every stroke
of her pen was smart and piquant. Her ideas
and feelings alternated rapidly from the most
earnest reasoning to childish vanity—from the
purest sentiments of friendship to the bitterness
of jealousy.

One thing, however, is certain—she worship-
ped the shrine of friendship with the most ardent
devotion. Alas! in some instances she reposed
too firm a confidence in it.

CHAPTER XVII.

DURING the season of 1830 Madame Malibran
performed in the Cenerentola, Romeo e Ju-
lietta, Otello, and Il Matrimonio Segreto. The
last-mentioned opera was brought out for the
benefit of Donzelli. Madame Malibran took
the character of Fidalma. She dressed the
part so well, and altogether presented such a

perfect personification of the character Cimarosa
intended, that her performance excited the
highest admiration.   She was dressed quite
in the old costume, and, throwing all coquetry
aside, she transformed herself into an old
woman.   The consequence was complete success.

In accepting the part of Romeo, after the
brilliant performance of the character by Pasta,
Malibran felt she was taking a bold step : she
nevertheless undertook it, and performed it
triumphantly.   Though fully aware of the difficulty of taking a character already pronounced
to be the *chef-d'œuvre* of another, yet she resolved to make the trial, and it was crowned
with success.

It was during this season (1830) that Maria
first made the acquaintance of Lablache, whose
high professional talents can only be equalled
by his private worth.

The acquaintance soon ripened into a cordial
friendship.   One day a poor Italian refugee

applied to Lablache for assistance. He had received permission to return home, but alas! he was destitute of the means. The next day, at rehearsal, Lablache broached the subject of the refugee's distress, and proposed a subscrip·tion. Madame Lablache, Donzelli, and several others, subscribed each two guineas. " And you, Maria," said Lablache, turning to Madame Malibran, " what will you give ?" " The same as the rest," answered she carelessly, and went on practising her part. With this little treasure the charitable and kind-hearted Lablache flew to succour his unfortunate countryman. The next morning Maria took an opportunity to speak to him alone. " Here are ten pounds more for your poor friend," said she, slipping a note into his hands : " I would not give more than the others yesterday, fearing they might think me ostentatious. Take it to him, but do not say a word about it to any one." Lablache joyfully hastened to the lodgings of the Italian refugee. He had left them, and had gone to embark. Nothing daunted, Lablache proceeded to the Tower stairs. The vessel was under weigh, and his friend on board. He hailed a boat, and offered the boatman a large reward, if he would row after the vessel, and overtake her. He succeeded in doing so. Lablache went on board, and presented the welcome donation to the refugee, who, falling on his knees, poured forth a heartfelt prayer for her who was thus ready to succour a fellow creature in distress.

CHAPTER XVIII.

Madame Malibran's occasional proneness to satire—Her prejudices and dislikes—Her description of a lady of rank—The
French Revolution—Early intimation of that event communicated to Madame Malibran—The fear of political troubles—The Duchess de Canizzaro's *soirée*—The Duke of
Wellington's flattering notice of Madame Malibran—Lucra-
tive engagements—Her power of enduring fatigue—Rapid
travelling—Reconciliation between Madame Malibran and
De Beriot—They leave London for Paris—Madame Malibran separates from Madame Naldi—Terms of her engagement in Paris.

MADAME MALIBRAN was sometimes extremely
satirical, and she was apt to conceive prejudices
and dislikes. Of this the following letter, written in the month of May, 1830, will afford some
proof.

" I dine to-morrow at Madame ——'s. What a strange woman she is ! Her manner of receiving me, though I brought a letter of recommendation from her daughter, was not less extraordinary than her mode of asking me to sing at four concerts for her. The remuneration she offered was so different from what I usually receive, that I was compelled rather to give her my services gratis, than stand bargaining with her for an hour.   Then she asked me to dinner to-morrow, thinking it a good set-off for my trouble.

" You know what an effect milk has when taken after oysters. This woman's look has precisely the same effect upon me. Her cold and disdainful air makes my blood curdle. I dread the idea of going there to-morrow. What an agreeable family dinner it will be !

" When I write, I fancy you are by my side, and that I am relating all my griefs to you. It appears to me that you are present—would to Heaven I were not mistaken ! Tell me, my

dear friend, whether I am rightly informed:
I have heard that we are about to have a second
edition of the French revolution. I long to
know whether there be any likelihood of its
success. If it should succeed, we shall probably have something of the same sort here;
in that case I may as well stay where I am.
I in vain try to elevate my ideas and become a
heroine; I confess myself a sad coward; I cannot get rid of my fears."

It is evident from the above letter that
Madame Malibran dreaded to visit France during the troubles of 1830. It appears that she
had obtained correct and early information of
the struggle about to take place. She treats
the subject in her usual style. Though looking
forward to the event as one to be dreaded, yet
she speaks of it with all the buoyant levity
which characterises her correspondence.

Her next letter shows how much importance
she attached to public applause.

" I did not dine with Madame ——. I really felt afraid of her, so I merely went in the evening; she, however, improves upon acquaintance. I sang for her, and afterwards went to the Duchess de Canizzaro's. Madame Lalande was there, but I was the object of all the *fanatisme.* The rooms were crowded, and the company mounted on chairs and tables to catch a glimpse of me. I never saw such enthusiasm. The Duke of Wellington came and shook hands with me: he is a delightful person. All the ladies present asked me to go and see them, and begged of me to give them my address, that they might call on me; in fact, you would have been enchanted had you seen their kindness towards your little girl, your spoiled pet.

" Adieu—I am off to a rehearsal of the ' Matrimonio Segreto,' which is to be performed on Saturday for Donzelli's benefit."

Though engaged at the opera, she made the

most of her time by singing at concerts in
London. This, though fatiguing, was highly
profitable to her.

On Wednesday, the 24th of May, she thus
wrote to a female friend.

" I must set off for Bath after the Concert
of Ancient Music. I shall arrive there at nine
in the morning, and at one o'clock start for
Bristol, where I am to perform with Donzelli in
the third act of Otello. I am to have one
hundred guineas for my trip, and shall return
on Thursday evening to London to sing at the
opera. This is hard but well-paid work."

In August she again visited Bath, and sang
at several concerts, receiving seventy-five pounds
for each performance. Having accidentally
heard that a concert was to be given at Calais
for the benefit of the poor, she instantly ordered
her carriage, started off, arrived there, sang

gratuitously, added a considerable donation to the receipts, and returned to England on the following morning.

Considering the delicacy of her frame, it is wonderful how she could bear up against these constant fatigues; but she had been early taught to despise what Garcia used to call *les faiblesses de la sexe*. She cheerfully encountered exertion and fatigue. Her moral courage overcame her physical weakness, and enabled her to achieve what more robust females would have feared to attempt.

But, amidst all her apparent gaiety, our heroine was deeply sensible to the unfortunate condition in which she was placed: deserted by her family, and separated from the man she loved, many were her hours of sorrow. She considered herself slighted by him for whom she had sacrificed all, yet still she could not banish his image from her breast. The following is a letter she wrote to a friend who had forwarded to her one from De Beriot, from whom she had not heard since their quarrel.

" May 1st, 1832.

" I have received your dear letter, with its enclosure . . . .

" It appears to me that it was very useless to address to you justifications which could be founded only on the errors of one who, on the other hand, conceives that she has a right to complain. Why seek excuses—why represent circumstances in an unfair point of view, for the purpose of self-justification? Might not that *person* be mistaken with respect to the opinions to which the journey would give rise? Had she not previously given sufficient proof that she more readily listened to the dictates of her heart than to those of her understanding? The objection, therefore, ought not to have arisen with her, but with one whose cooler judgment was better enabled to calculate consequences.

" If you had not read the letter yourself, you might have been misled. But, thank Heaven, you know the whole affair !

" As to *ton amie*, she wept like a child, on perusing the letter you enclosed. She thought that *perhaps* she had suffered her warmth of temper to betray her too far—that perhaps she did not know him well enough to judge him—that perhaps—in short I cannot tell how many foolish ideas occurred to her. However, I can assure you that she did not sleep a wink during the whole of the night, and in the morning her pale face sufficiently denoted the painful subject which had occupied her thoughts. . . . . But I will say no more on this subject. . . . . This evening I perform in the third act of *Romeo e Giulietta*."

The above letter, in spite of its obscurity, indicates that a reconciliation between Madame Malibran and De Beriot was not far distant.

Accordingly, a short time after the letter was

written, De Beriot arrived in London, and he
and Madame Malibran set out together for
Paris.

Soon after her arrival there, Madame Malibran separated from Madame Naldi, and took
up her abode in a small house which she had
hired in the Rue Blanche.

She entered into an engagement with Severini and Robert, the new directors of the Théâtre Italien.   The terms were 1175 francs for
each performance.

CHAPTER XIX.

Differences between Madame Malibran and the directors of the
Opera—Imprudent disregard of her health—Evil consequences of her over-exertions—Fainting-fit—Unlucky mistake—The manager's dilemma—A desperate remedy—
Madame Malibran's frequent use of restoratives—False re-
ports on this subject—Her indifference to pain and exhaustion.

DURING this season Madame Malibran did not
appear in any new characters, but she was
more than ever admired in her old parts. She
was ably seconded by Mademoiselle Sontag.
Between these two charming singers there was
a constant struggle for pre-eminence, a desire
to outvie each other, which gave a spur to their

exertions, and nightly attracted crowds to hear them.

Madame Malibran was continually at variance with the directors of the Opera. They remonstrated with her on the little regard she paid to the preservation of her health, and the probable injury her voice would incur from her fondness for every species of amusement. Unlike other singers, she never spared herself. On all occasions she was ready to volunteer her services. She amused herself with riding, dancing, and all sorts of violent exercises, and her fondness for late hours was highly prejudicial to her vocal powers.

One evening she had promised me her company at an evening party. The managers unexpectedly determined that a benefit at which she was bound to perform should take place that night. Madame Malibran remonstrated, but in vain. Monsieur Robert was obdurate, " Well," said Maria, " make what arrangement you please : I will be at the theatre because it is my duty, but I'll go to Madame Merlin's because it is my pleasure !"

She kept her word. After playing Semiramide she came to my house, sang three songs, ate a hearty supper, and waltzed till long after the dawn of day.

She did not, however, always escape the ill consequences of this imprudence, though the public were little aware of the state of suffering under which she appeared before them. On one occasion, having passed the whole night at a ball, on her return home, finding she had to play that evening, she retired to bed and slept till noon. On rising, she ordered her saddle-horse, galloped off, returned home at six, partook of a hurried dinner, and away to the Opera, where she was to play Arsace. Having dressed for the part, she was about to announce her readiness, when, overcome by exhaustion, she fell down in a fainting-fit. In an instant the alarm spread, and assistance was summoned. Twenty different remedies were tried, twenty bottles of perfume and other restoratives proffered, and among others a bottle of hartshorn. In the confusion of the moment, Monsieur Robert (who was terrified out of his senses by this unfortunate occurrence) unluckily seized the hartshorn, and applied it to the lips instead of the nose of the fainting prima donna. Madame Malibran recovered, but alas! the hartshorn had frightfully blistered her lips. Here was an unforeseen misfortune ; the house was already filled—the audience were beginning to manifest impatience. It was now too late to change the performance—Monsieur Robert knew not what apology to offer. " Stay," exclaimed Madame Malibran, " I'll remedy this." Taking up a pair of scissors, she approached the looking-glass, and, though suffering the most acute pain, she cut from her lips the skin which had been raised by the blisters. In ten minutes afterwards she was on the stage singing with Semiramide-Sontag.

It has often been said that she indulged in the

use of strong spirits ; that, in short, she was addicted to intemperate drinking. This was a mistake, arising from her occasional use of tonics. To these she had recourse when her failing strength required artificial stimulus. When nature refused to assist her, which was frequently the case, she would fly to these restoratives. She would sometimes take a glass of Madeira to renovate her voice, and enable her to accomplish her fatiguing tasks. It was not any partiality for strong drinks. Could vinegar have produced the same effect, she would have flown to it. To accomplish her triumphs, she set physical force at defiance : nothing daunted her. In the instance above mentioned, her lacerated and bleeding lips caused her to suffer severe pain throughout the whole opera. To gratify her audience at Manchester, she sang three times the duet from *Andromica* within a few hours of her death —a death caused by extreme and unceasing exertions.

CHAPTER XX.

Garcia engages himself at the opera in Paris—Alteration in
his voice—Madame Malibran's fears for her father's failure
—Garcia's extraordinary musical talent—Anecdote related
by Madame Rossini—Musical *tour de force.*

GARCIA, who had for some time past retired
from public performance, now accepted an engagement offered to him by the managers of the
Italian Opera in Paris. This annoyed his daughter very much. His once fine tenor voice had
become a barritone, and he could no longer
touch those parts originally written for him.
Madame Malibran trembled for him. She
knew the unbending spirit of her father, which,
like her own, struggled against every obstacle;

she also knew that his pride would rebel against declining any character proposed to him. She therefore feared that, by some signal failure, he might forfeit those laurels which his former talents had so triumphantly won.

One evening she felt particularly anxious and uneasy. Her father had accepted a part which she well knew he was unfitted for. It was not within the compass of his voice. It was beyond the power he then possessed; but still she dared not say a word to him. In the greatest trepidation she entered her box. A sudden hoarseness attacked him shortly before he proceeded to the theatre. " No matter," said he, " I will contrive to get through my part." And he did get through it admirably. By the ready exercise of that musical talent with which he was so eminently gifted, he adapted the part to the state of his voice, transposing to an octave lower those passages which were too high for him, and adroitly taking the written notes where they came within the compass of his voice. The promptitude and accuracy with which he performed these changes were truly surprising.

The following anecdote affords a still more striking example of Garcia's musical talent: it was told to me by Madame Rossini, (then Mademoiselle Colbran,) as the most extraordinary instance of musical power she had ever heard of.

Mademoiselle Colbran and Garcia were both engaged at Naples. A new opera was to be produced, and Garcia very much disliked the part allotted to him. He neglected to study it, and made a boast of being totally ignorant of it. At length, after a dozen preparatory rehearsals, during which he had merely looked it over, the day of the final rehearsal arrived. Garcia attended, but, alas! not one note, not one word of his part, had he learned.

Mademoiselle Colbran was in despair. "For heaven's sake!" she said, "let us get this piece put off. If you are so imperfect, we shall all be hissed."

" Don't alarm yourself," replied Garcia; " I
will get over the difficulty.   Of course you
know your own part ?"

" Certainly," answered the lady.

" Well, then," said he, turning to the
prompter, " think of nobody but me ; give me
out the words distinctly, and as to the music,
that's my affair."

Far from being satisfied, poor Mademoiselle
Colbran never slept that night.   She almost
fainted with agitation next evening when she
saw Garcia come on the stage.   He had acknowledged that he had not learned a single
note of the part he was about to undertake.
What, then, was her surprise when, with cool
confidence, he sang a beautiful cavatina, and
having finished it commenced a well-arranged
recitative, and joined in several concerted
pieces ?   In short, he went through the whole
opera with unbounded applause, but without
giving *one note of the composer's music.*

The fact was, during the rehearsals he had

attentively studied the harmonies of the accompaniments. Having made himself thoroughly acquainted with them, he was enabled to substitute for the part which the composer had assigned to him, one of his own adaptation, improvising, as he proceeded, in the most extraordinary manner possible.

Madame Rossini always mentioned this as the most astonishing example of musical talent and facility that had ever come under her notice.

CHAPTER XXI.

Madame Malibran performs Otello instead of Desdemona—
Representation of male characters by women—Madame
Malibran visits England and Brussels—She breaks off her
engagement in Paris—Perplexity of the managers of the
opera — Intercession of M. Viardot— Madame Malibran
returns to keep her engagement in Paris—Her sudden
refusal to perform—Cause of her indisposition—She forfeits
some degree of her popularity.

AT the close of the season Madame Malibran
chose the opera of " Otello " for her benefit.
With the view of presenting a novelty, she was
induced to personate the Moor, instead of the
gentle Desdemona; but, like a similar attempt
made by Madame Pasta in London, the result
was a decided failure.

The small and feminine form of Madame Malibran was in no respect adapted to the manly and heroic character of Otello. The dusky colour, too, with which she tinged her countenance, not only deformed the beauty of her features, but concealed all that flexibility of expression which was their peculiar charm. If in contralto parts the public have sometimes tolerated the representation of male characters by women, it is only because they have not previously seen those same characters personated by men.

In the spring, Madame Malibran returned to London, and played the whole season on the same terms as usual; she also sang in several concerts at Bath, Bristol, and Manchester, passed a few weeks at Brussels, and returned to Paris in the latter end of September.

But previously to the opening of the opera in Paris, her delicate state of health induced her to write to M. Severini, stating her determination to relinquish her engagement, and, without waiting another moment, she started for Brussels.

This intimation filled the directors of the Opera with dismay. They found themselves suddenly placed in a most difficult dilemma. To supply Malibran's place was impossible. She had a part in almost every piece; it was therefore equally impossible to do without her. To have closed the theatre would have been ruinous to all connected with it. What was to be done? They held counsel together, but they could come to no satisfactory conclusion. At length it was proposed to try what could be effected by the intercession of a friend. At the earnest solicitation of the managers, M. Viardot proceeded to Brussels, to use his influence with the capricious cantatrice. At first she was inexorable, but after some persuasion, and a fair representation of the injustice she was doing to the establishment, to the public, and to herself, she suddenly started up—" You are right; I see now that I have acted inconsiderately; but

when I resolved to leave Paris I was very miserable. Come, let us be off quickly." In a few
hours she was again on her way to Paris.

On her arrival, she entered into new terms
with the managers, by which she was to be
allowed to retire before the close of the season.
Her health, however, still continued precarious;
and this circumstance injured her much in
public opinion. It frequently happened that
when an opera was advertised, and people had
already secured boxes, bills were pasted at the
doors, announcing that, in consequence of the
sudden indisposition of Madame Malibran, the
opera was unavoidably changed. The next
evening she was perhaps well, and played with
more than her accustomed spirit. The consequence was, she was looked upon as uncertain
and capricious, and she forfeited some share of
the popularity she formerly possessed.

She, on her part, became irritable, her good
spirits deserted her, and her whole manner
appeared to change. One evening, when she

was playing Arsace, towards the close of the first act she found herself unwell. On leaving the stage she proceeded to her dressing-room, and locking herself up, declared that she would play no more that night. Entreaty and remonstrance were equally vain; and the manager found it no easy matter to appease the dissatisfaction of the audience, the majority of whom regarded the indisposition as feigned. No doubt it was in part attributable to her keen susceptibility of feeling. She was at that time *enceinte*, and the idea of her dishonour haunted her. She imagined that everybody was aware of her situation, and she became gloomy and fretful. She nevertheless persevered in performing as long as she was able, hoping thereby to mislead curiosity and conjecture.

CHAPTER XXII.

Coolness of Madame Malibran's former friends—Her father
and the Countess de Sparre refuse to see her—A dishonour-
able suggestion — Madame Malibran's indignation — Her
wounded feelings—General Lafayette interests himself to
obtain her divorce — Legal discussions — Informality in
the performance of the marriage ceremony—Garcia reconciled to his daughter—Joyful feeling excited by that circumstance—Madame Malibran's letter to the Countess de Merlin
—De Beriot and his violin.

MADAME MALIBRAN soon began to feel the
change of her position in society. Those who
had formerly courted her now shunned her, or
merely invited her in her professional capacity.
Her father, too, refused to see her, and Madame
de Sparre, the friend whom of all others she

most esteemed, closed her doors against her.
This was the most severe blow of all ; and
though her extraordinary talents still continued
to win unbounded applause in public, yet her
private moments were embittered by the slights
of those who once respected her.

Under these circumstances several friends
advised her to return to her husband, promising
their countenance and support if she would
do so.

" What ! hide my fault at the price of such an
act of baseness? Never ! it were far better to
avow my dishonour and suffer for it."

One evening she came to a musical party at
my house. Just as she was approaching the
piano for the purpose of singing the duet in
Semiramide, " Eh ben, a te ferisce," she cast
her eyes on a lady who had formerly been her
friend, but who now looked coldly on her.
Madame Malibran turned pale. Her eyes
overflowed with tears, and turning to me, she
murmured, " Not a look, not the slightest sign

of recognition from one who once so sincerely loved me. She considers me unworthy of her notice."

" Courage, Maria," replied I in a whisper ; " do not thus give way to your feelings : when the concert is over, we'll see what can be done."

This assurance soothed her, and she went through the duet, though in evident distress. After the concert I spoke to Madame ——, who, at my request, consented to exchange a few words with poor Maria. She, however. confined herself to terms of cold civility, and no further reconciliation could be brought about.

Her mortified feelings, and the endeavours she made to conceal her situation, rendered her truly an object of pity. Compelled nightly to appear before the public, and often forced to hear the most coarse remarks, she took a dislike to that profession which had hitherto been to her a source of pleasure.

Her thoughts now reverted with redoubled force to the one all-absorbing hope of her future life—I allude to the legal separation which she had long sought from her husband; this, however, was not now sufficient; a divorce became absolutely necessary, though it was a step attended with much difficulty. The French courts refused to take cognisance of formalities gone through in America, while the tribunals of that country declared their inability to interfere, since the marriage had not been contracted according to the laws of the United States.

In vain did her good old friend General Lafayette pore over the statutes of the two nations, in the hope of finding some precedent that would be applicable to her case. Many distinguished members of the French bar exerted all their ingenuity in endeavouring to discover some informality which might furnish ground for a divorce.

At length the following plan was thought of. Monsieur Malibran was a native of France, yet, on establishing himself in America, he had demanded and obtained letters of naturalisation. The act which conferred on him the privileges of a citizen of the United States set forth that in receiving those privileges he renounced his character of a Frenchman. On the other hand, Maria Garcia, being the daughter of a Spaniard, who had obtained letters of naturalisation in France, was, though born in Paris, really a Spanish subject. Thus the facts of the case were simply as follows : two foreigners, the one an American and the other a Spaniard, had presented themselves to the French consul at New York to be married ; and the consul, supposing these two foreigners to be two French subjects, had married them.

It next became a question whether the French courts of law could adjudge between two foreigners; but to this objection it was urged that Monsieur and Madame Malibran had, subsequently to their marriage, both returned;

that the former had claimed his right as a
citizen of France, and had thereby empowered
the French tribunals to decide upon his case.
Let us now leave the legal proceedings to
pursue their tardy course, and return to Madame
Malibran.

At this period of anxiety and distress, Garcia
relented; he became once more reconciled to
his child. Maria's joy on this occasion is best
told in a note I received from her, in answer to
an invitation I had sent her to come and sing
at my house.

" With the greatest pleasure I promise to
come to you to-night. I am so happy! Everything has gone well with me since yesterday.
This reconciliation is a good omen. I was sure
a kind friend like you would rejoice to hear it.
As soon as *he* comes in, I shall show him your
dear note, and I am sure he will put his violin
into his pocket, and attend you with the

greatest pleasure. Adieu—I embrace you with all my heart. I shall try to be with you by nine, or even earlier.

" MARIA,

" Que sus bellos y dulces carrillos
besa con amor y respeto.*

* Who kisses your sweet cheeks with love and respect.

CHAPTER XXIII.

Kind mediation of General Mina—Madame Malibran's last
performance in Paris—The notes of the dying swan—
Malibran's departure for Brussels—Her return to Paris in
disguise—Her accouchement—Resolves not to sing again
in pubilc till she is married to De Beriot—An unexpected
visit from Lablache—Madame Malibran's sudden departure
for Italy—Her passport—Her performance at Rome—Unfavourable reception—French romances.

GENERAL MINA, a friend of Garcia's family,
had greatly contributed, by his kind mediation,
to bring about the reconciliation between the
father and daughter. Madame Malibran felt
most grateful to him. But her bosom was still
a prey to a thousand conflicting pangs. She
felt she was losing public favour in Paris.

Her once enraptured audiences now listened to her mellifluous tones in almost frigid silence. The newspaper critics began to be severe and unjust. A spirit like Madame Malibran's could not brook this. Some weeks prior to the close of the season she announced her farewell benefit, which took place on the 8th of January.

The opera she chose was Otello. On this memorable evening she sang in her very finest style, as if to make the Parisians remember her with the deeper regret. Alas! they then heard her for the last time. She exerted herself to the utmost, and she was sublime. The audience were enthusiastic in their applause. The gentlemen stood on the benches and cheered her; ladies waved their handkerchiefs, and threw garlands on the stage. With shouts of admiration were mingled expressions of regret for her departure. But her wings were already spread; her last notes, like the dying swan, rang in their ears.

Next morning she started for Brussels, accompanied only by her waiting-maid.   She remained but a few hours in that city.   With the assistance of De Beriot she provided herself with a complete disguise, and a peruke of light hair rendered it quite impossible to recognise her.   She then instantly returned to Paris, and took up her abode in a retired house, situated at the end of the Rue des Martyrs. There she remained concealed for nearly two months.   As soon as she was sufficiently recovered from her accouchement to be enabled to travel, she once more set off for Brussels.

In the company of the man she loved, she tried to forget her past sorrows, and to banish them by mingling in a continual round of amusements.

On leaving the French metropolis, Maria Malibran had secretly vowed never again to sing in public till she was the wife of De Beriot. She had now accumulated 600,000 francs, (24,000*l.*) having performed three seasons in

Paris, and two in London. She was therefore sufficiently independent to be able to abide by her determination.

Subsequent circumstances, however, tempted her to alter her resolve, as the sequel will show. About the middle of July, Lablache visited Brussels, on his way to Naples, and hearing by accident that Madame Malibran was in that city, he immediately called upon her, though he had only a few hours to stay. It was eight in the evening when he made his visit; Madame Malibran was delighted to see him, and pressed him to stay.

" It is impossible," replied Lablache ; " I must retire to bed early, being compelled to start at daybreak on my journey."

" And why should not I go with you ?" said she ; " I have no other engagement. Yes, I am resolved I'll go with you."

" Then you must be very speedy, for most positively I must be off by six o'clock."

" Never mind—I'll be ready."

Lablache, conceiving this to be a mere joke, laughingly wished her good-night and returned to his hotel.

In the morning, about five o'clock, he was startled by hearing a post-carriage drive up to his door. He jumped up, thinking it was the conveyance he had ordered, and he felt annoyed at having overslept himself. He opened the windows to look out, and Madame Malibran's voice greeted—" Come, Lablache, I'm ready and waiting for you."

Lablache was thunderstruck; he could scarcely believe his eyes. That a resolution should be thus taken so suddenly, and every arrangement made for so long a journey in so short a time, appeared like a dream. For a few moments he fancied he must be mistaken. In half an hour afterwards they were on their way to Italy.

On arriving at the Italian frontier Madame Malibran recollected for the first time that she required a passport, which in the hurry of her departure she had quite forgotten. She was

therefore obliged to remain behind whilst Lablache went forward, and having detailed the
circumstances to the authorities at Milan,
he obtained permission for her to enter Lom-
bardy.

She did not, however, stay long in Lom-
bardy, but hastened on to Rome, where she
made an engagement for four nights. She was,
however, but indifferently received; she had
the bad taste to sing *two French romances* in
the scene of the music lesson in the " Barbiere,"
which the Romans looked upon as an ill-timed
pleasantry, and they showed their sense of it.

CHAPTER XXIV.

Madame Malibran's engagement at Naples—Jealousy of Madame Ronzi de Begnis—Malibran's acting in the last scene of Desdemona—Donzelli—Madame Malibran's *début* at the Fondo Theatre—Immense crowd on that occasion—She performs in the Cenerentola and the Gazza Ladra—Her interview with the king of Naples—Her extraordinary request to his majesty—The King applauds her on her first appearance—Public performers in Italy—Madame Malibran rides on horseback—Aquatic excursions in the Bay of Naples—Imprudent bathing.

DURING her stay in Rome, Madame Malibran received information of the death of her father. She was so deeply afflicted by the event, that she kept her bed for several days. On this melancholy occasion she wrote a letter to Monsieur Viardot, expressive of her deep sorrow.* Whilst she was in Rome she signed an engagement with Barbaja, the director of the opera at Naples, for twelve nights performance in that city, on very advantageous terms.   To fulfil this contract she left Rome, but on her arrival in Naples she found that Madame Ronzi de Begnis was already in possession of all her parts at San Carlos, where she was a prodigious favourite, and refused to cede them to the new comer.   The consequence was, Madame Malibran made her first curtsey to a Neapolitan audience at the Fondo Theatre, on the 6th of August, in the character of Desdemona. At this theatre she performed ten of the twelve nights for which she had been engaged for San Carlos.

Barbaja, who had the direction of both the establishments, wisely calculated that as almost all the boxes at San Carlos were already let, Madame Malibran could add but little to his

* See Appendix.

receipts there, whereas her appearance at the Fondo would be sure to draw large sums of money to his treasury.

Here she obtained the most signal success. She introduced the aria from Donna Caritea in her first scene in Otello, and from that to the closing scene in the opera her acting and singing produced the most electrifying effect upon the audience.

The Neapolitans had hitherto seen this scene tamely performed, or altogether omitted. Madame Malibran was the first who truly depicted to them the sufferings of Desdemona. In the dying scene, the manner in which she endeavoured to escape the fate which an instant before she had invoked, was almost too forcible a representation of reality.

I remember once a friend advising her not to make Othello pursue her so long when he was about to kill her: her answer was, " You are right, it is not elegant, I admit ; but when once I fairly enter into my character, I never think of effects, but I imagine myself really the person I represent. I can assure you that in the last scene of Desdemona I often feel as if I were really about to be murdered, and act accordingly."

Donzelli used to be much annoyed by Madame Malibran not determining beforehand how he was to seize her: she often gave him a regular chase. Though he was one of the best-tempered men in the world, I recollect seeing him one evening seriously angry. Desdemona had, according to custom, repeatedly escaped from his grasp. In pursuing her he stumbled, and slightly wounded himself with the dagger he grasped. It was the only time I ever saw him in a passion. But to return to Madame Malibran's *début* at the Fondo.

On that evening the crowd was so great that the Russian and Austrian ambassadors (Count Stackelberg and Lebzellern) could not obtain places : as a great favour, they at last found

room in the fourth tier opposite the grand
lustre, which, out of respect to them, was
drawn higher up, to enable them to catch a
glimpse of the *débutante*.

A few nights afterwards she played in the
Cenerentola. She was not much applauded,
except in the variations of the finale, which
were warmly admired. She therefore never
again appeared in that opera.

Neither were the Neapolitans altogether
pleased with her in the Gazza Ladra. Her
acting in the quintette scene was thought to
partake too much of tragic dignity for a peasant,
who, whatever her grief might be, could never
have thus suddenly acquired an elegance beyond
her humble lot.

The rule of Naples is, that when an actress
is about to make her *début*, she waits on the
king, and solicits the honour of his majesty's
presence on her first appearance. In compli-
ance with this regulation, Madame Malibran
went to the palace, where she was received most
graciously.

On being introduced to the king, she said, hesitatingly, " Sire, if it be agreeable to your majesty, I have come to request that your majesty will be graciously pleased *not* to appear at the theatre to-morrow evening."

The king, not a little astonished, demanded the reason of a request so singular.

" May it please your majesty, I have heard that it is the etiquette in Naples not to applaud in presence of royalty : that is to say, unless you graciously set the example."

The king, perceiving that she was embarrassed, desired her to speak out.

" Sire, as you are good enough to command me to speak, I will. The fact is, I am so much in the habit of being applauded the instant I appear on the stage, that I am sure, if I were received in silence, I couldn't sing a note."

" Very well," said his majesty, " I will set the example. Fear not; you shall be abundantly applauded."

Madame Malibran returned home highly

satisfied by having thus secured powerful protection. In the evening, just before she made
her appearance on the stage, she got between
the side-scenes, where she might be seen from
the royal box, and having caught the eye of
the king, reminded him of his promise by
clapping her hands. His majesty, pleased with
her freedom and originality, failed not to be as
good as his word, and the whole house loudly
responded to the royal signal.

On the 7th of September she performed at
San Carlos, in the character of Rosina in the
Barbiere, and Romeo in the third act of Romeo
e Giulietta. She was rapturously admired in
both these characters, but the last-mentioned
opera was by no means popular.

The Neapolitans are fond of musical novelty,
and it was scarcely to be expected that they
would listen with pleasure to an opera which
had been performed every season during ten
consecutive years.

During the fêtes of St. Januarius, (in September,) Madame Malibran took advantage of the temporary close of the theatre to visit Rome, where she played three times, and returned to finish her engagement at Naples.

In Italy public performers are not so well received as in England and France. They are, it is true, highly admired, applauded, and asked to all the leading parties; but they are appreciated merely for their talents, and are never admitted to that equality, that intimacy which is sometimes even more gratifying than pecuniary reward Madame Malibran felt this acutely; and she endeavoured, as much as possible, to shun those who affected to look down upon her. During her abode in Naples she sought, amidst the varied charms which Nature has conferred on this favoured spot, to amuse herself, without risking the slights to which she was exposed in Neapolitan society.

Her mornings were usually spent on horseback. She would gallop over the lovely plains of the surrounding country, or climb the rugged

sides of Mount Vesuvius. At other times she
would row in the Bay by moonlight. This was
one of her favourite amusements; for hours she
would thus float on the waves, singing some of
her favourite strains, delighted to hear the
effect of her voice on the water. This, though
imprudent, was not half so perilous to her
health as her frequent habit of bathing at an
hour when the sun's power is so great that few
of the inhabitants of Naples will venture from
their houses—and this, too, while she was in
a delicate state of health. But she seldom
looked forward to consequences, when the
whim of the moment was to be gratified.

CHAPTER XXV.

The King of Naples and Madame Ronzi de Begnis—Madame Malibran leaves Naples to fulfil an engagement at Bologna—Bolognese society—Gratifying reception of Madame Malibran—She is engaged to perform at Milan—Proposes to cancel her engagement—She secretly quits Milan, and proceeds to Brussels—Birth of her second child.

HAVING played two or three nights beyond the number stipulated in her engagement, Madame Malibran demanded an increased salary, which the manager refusing, she signed an agreement with Azzolini, the director of the theatre at Bologna. On the whole, it may be said that Madame Malibran was not successful at

I 2

Naples. This may be inferred from the following passage in a letter I received from her a few days before she quitted that city.

" I have succeeded well here. I have every reason to believe the Neapolitans appreciate my talent, but they seldom applaud me. This will never do: applause to an actress is like warmth to life—it is a necessity. How can one sing without it? You will perhaps ask, were they deaf? No. Did I sing badly? Far from it. It is merely because I am *too thin.**

" Do you understand me now? No. So much the worse, then, for I'll give you no further explanation. * * * * *

" I still regret my absence from Paris; but I will never return till I am married to De Beriot. Not that I fear the public, whom I have always

* The meaning of this is, that the king had ceased to applaud Madame Malibran, which she fancied arose from Madame de Begnis being under his protection. Madame de Begnis was at that time very stout.

found kind and indulgent, but on account of my friends and relations," &c. &c.

Madame Malibran arrived about the middle of October at Bologna, and was received with the greatest approbation in " Romeo," " Otello,' and " Tancredi."

The society of Bologna was highly agreeable, and their reception of her most flattering. Of all the cities in Italy it is perhaps the most delightful. There the nobility and gentry mingle, without those petty jealousies which the presence of a court gives rise to. Hospitality and kindness are not dependent on the smiles of a prince, or the private likings or dislikings of some upstart ambassador, who, in a greater city, may choose to stamp with the hand of patronage or exclusion some temporary sojourner far better born than himself. In Bologna birth and talent are the only two letters of recommendation ; possess either, and you are sure to be welcome.

But to return to my subject. Some of the scenes in the Capuletti were given in a style which perfectly entranced the audience; while Madame Malibran's acting in the Somnambula produced such an effect that she was called *twice* on the stage, after the curtain had fallen, to receive the congratulations of the audience. She was accompanied home from the theatre in a sort of triumph. Her residence was actually surrounded till daybreak by the enraptured Bolognese.

After her engagement in that city she was engaged to perform at Milan, her first appearance being fixed for the 12th of December. She was now for the second time *enceinte,* and this circumstance induced her to propose to the managers to cancel her engagement. This, however, they would not hear of; so, to get rid of their entreaties, and to escape from the fines which she would have been compelled to pay, Madame Malibran at once set out for

Brussels, where she arrived in safety, after a most fatiguing journey. She gave birth to her second child in the month of January, 1833.

CHAPTER XXVI.

As soon as Madame Malibran was sufficiently
recovered, she started for London; but, being
attacked by a severe sore-throat, she was for
some time in doubt whether she would be

able to appear. However, by the aid of Dr. Belloumini, she was in a few hours miraculously cured of this alarming illness, and was enabled in a few days to make her *début* on the English stage. She was engaged for the season at Drury Lane theatre, at the rate of £150 per night!

The interest she excited amply repaid the managers. All London flocked to hear her. Her appearance in the Somnambula, which was translated into English expressly for her, formed an epoch in the annals of the English drama, and to obtain a place in the theatre on the nights of her performance was regarded as a prize. After the run of this piece she sang in a revived opera called " The Devil's Bridge," which was followed by a new opera by Chelard. She also sang at concerts, and during a temporary close of the theatre she made a profitable tour through England, receiving large sums for performing at musical festivals and benefit concerts.

Having amassed a considerable sum, she again returned to Brussels, where she sang, not only in public, but twice at the palace. Many blamed the selection of her music on these occasions. It consisted of mere ballads, far too trivial to please those who came expecting to be astonished. But Madame Malibran was always capricious: such is the only excuse I can offer for her thus trifling with public favour.

Renewed engagements demanded her presence in Italy. She again started for Naples on the 8th of November, 1833, and played there in Otello on the 14th of the same month. But a peculiar circumstance marred the success of her appearance on this occasion. The superstition of the Neapolitans is proverbial; they entertain the most invincible horror of the *cattiva sorte*, and ascribe to that evil genius the most unbounded influence.

It happened that the 14th of November was a grand gala day in Naples. Otello was an-

nounced for the *début* of Madame Malibran;
but, in deference to public feeling, it was deemed
necessary to insert the following notice in the
bill: " E per non funestar una cosi lieta ricor-
renza, il terzo. atto non sarà rappresentato." *
Consequently Madame Malibran was deprived
of the brilliant triumph she had a right to
expect from her powerful acting in the dying
scene. She subsequently performed in the
Prova and the Gazza Ladra, but she was received with less enthusiasm than that which
had greeted her at the Fondo. The subscribers to San Carlos felt a little pique against
her for having, as they supposed, on her previous visit to Naples, preferred the second
theatre to theirs. But this was a mistake: in
performing at the Fondo Theatre, she merely
acceded to the arrangements made by the managers. Paccini had just composed a new opera
expressly for her, entitled " Irene." It was

* To banish evil augury on this happy occasion, the third
act will not be performed.

played, for the first time, on the 30th of November, and was instantly withdrawn. Madame
Malibran sang in her very best style a fine duet
with her sister, Mademoiselle Garcia, and exerted herself in every way, but in vain ; the
critics condemned the opera, to rise no
more.

In Semiramide and Romeo she was also
received coldly. In the former opera she offended by introducing several compositions of
Mercadante and Vaccai, and in the latter the
feelings of the audience were outraged by the
funeral procession of Giulietta: they rose en
masse, and hissed it off the stage.

On the 19th of January, 1834, she again
appeared in a new opera by Coccia, entitled
" *La Figlia del aria :*" it only lived three
nights.

Weary of trying new characters and failing
in them, Madame Malibran again resorted to
her old favourite, " Il Matrimonio Segreto," in
which she played Fidalma. The Neapoli-

tans, however, determined to be dissatisfied, condemned her for thus personating an old woman, and disapproved of her disfiguring her pretty face.

To compensate for these professional disappointments, Madame Malibran devoted herself during the day to every sort of rural enjoyment. Pic-nic water parties, and excursions to explore the beauties of the country in the environs of Naples, were her constant recreations. On one of these occasions, when returning by water from Pausillipo, she took it into her head, on arriving at the line of rocks near the Castel del Nuovo, to jump out of the boat, and to spring from rock to rock, to gain the mainland. This feat was attended by no little danger, and she was several times up to her waist in water. One single false step might have been fatal to her; yet, in the careless mood of the moment, she laughed at the fears of her friends, and looked upon the perilous attempt as an amusing frolic

Her operatic triumph she reserved for the close of her engagement.   On the 23rd of February, 1834, she played Norma, and by her splendid acting produced such a sensation, that the audience, as if to make atonement for former coldness, rose and cheered her for several minutes.

For many days nothing was talked of but Malibran; the Neapolitans forgot all other singers in the admiration they felt for her.   But Maria Malibran was not to be so easily won. They had offended her—deeply offended her; she had now convinced them of their error, but determined to give them no further opportunity of undervaluing her merits.   She quitted Naples on the 13th of March, leaving behind her a reputation for musical talent seldom equalled and never surpassed.

CHAPTER XXVII.

Madame Malibran's appearance at Milan—Recollections of Pasta—The acting of Pasta and Malibran compared—Madame Malibran revisits England, to fulfil her professional engagements—Returns to Milan and Sinigaglia—The Château of d'Aucy le Franc—Surprise of the Marquis de Louvois—Illness of Madame Malibran—The Italian ballad-singer—Charity judiciously applied.

ON her arrival at Milan, Madame Malibran had to struggle against the impression which Pasta had left behind her in those same characters she was about to assume. For the first few evenings she found the Milanese faithful to their late favourite, but when she appeared in Norma she completely eclipsed her predecessor, and was universally pronounced to be the *cantante par excellenza.* On a comparison of Malibran and Pasta, the difference between these two gifted persons was obvious. Pasta was the perfection of art and study; her every movement was correct and graceful; but, after seeing her perform once, you might easily know on a future evening what you were to expect. Having once laid down the rules of her action, she never varied from them. She was always delightful, but always the same.

Malibran, on the other hand, was a child of nature. Her gestures, her attitudes, varied according to the feelings of the moment. She never laid down any studied points. She came upon the stage, entered heart and soul into the personation, and allowed her feelings entirely to guide her.

The superior reception she met with at Milan, at a time when the public memory was vividly impressed with the performance of one of the finest actresses that ever trod the stage, is a convincing proof that nature, even in her wildest moods, is always more pleasing than the most masterly efforts of art.

Having played twenty nights, Madame Malibran suddenly left Milan for the purpose of fulfilling her engagements in England, but not before she had signed an agreement with Duke Visconti (the director of La Scala) to return there as soon as she was again free.

In England she merely remained her promised time, and then returned to Italy, having agreed with Signor Azzolini to sing at Sinigaglia during the fair held in that town. She was to perform fifteen times between the 15th of July and the 11th of August.

In the course of her journey, as she was passing the Château d'Aucy le Franc, she felt a wish to see the park. It was only six o'clock in the morning, and she thought she might enter it unobserved. She accordingly alighted from her carriage with De Beriot. They were enjoying the stroll, when the proprietor of the domain (the Marquis de Louvois) met

them. For a moment Madame Malibran endeavoured to shun him, and even attempted
to run away; but coming directly up to Monsieur de Beriot, whom he had formerly known
the Marquis begged to be introduced to his
boyish companion, for Madame Malibran was, ·
according to her frequent custom, disguised in
male attire. She wore a pair of loose trowsers
and a blouse. The surprise of the Marquis
may be easily imagined when he discovered who
the supposed boy really was. The Marquis ur-
gently pressed them to stay and spend a few days
on his estate, but they were unable to accept his
invitation. Madame Malibran in her turn invited the Marquis to come and visit her in
Naples at the end of the year.

Madame Malibran arrived in safety at Sinigaglia. During the latter part of the journey
she seated herself on the coachbox and drove,
though the sun was scorchingly hot. Within a
few minutes after she dismounted from the box,
she plunged into the sea to bathe. This im-

prudence threw her into a violent fit of illness:
she was seized with fever, and her voice became
suddenly hoarse. Imagining that this was the
mere effect of weakness, and determined not to
yield to it, she drank a glass or two of cham-
pagne, and thereby made herself worse. A
doctor was called in, and it was supposed she
would be unable to appear for several weeks;
the manager therefore selected a sort of secunda
prima donna, who filled up the vacancy until our
heroine became convalescent. Thanks to a good
constitution, her illness was not of long duration.
She made her *début* in Norma, and filled
the audience with delight and admiration. One
evening, during her stay at Sinagaglia, she
heard a beggar woman singing beneath the
window of her hotel. Being struck with the
beauty of the woman's voice, she sent for her,
and questioned her about her family, &c. Finding that it was not idleness, but real want, had
driven the poor creature to her wandering way
of life, Madame Malibran made provision for

enabling the woman to receive a course of
musical instruction. She placed her under a
good master, and paid for her musical education, till death deprived the poor ballad-singer
of her liberal patroness.

CHAPTER XXVIII.

Madame Malibran proceeds to Lucca—She is compelled to sing on the market-place of Sinigaglia—Curious scene—Admiration of the populace—Persiani's Ines de Castro—The Ducal court—Gallantry of the Duke and his nobles—New engagement at Milan and Naples—The finale in the Somnambula—Extraordinary example of vocal execution—Madame Malibran's dislike to the character of Tancredi—The French hairdresser.

On the 13th of August, Madame Malibran started for Lucca. In passing through the market-place of Sinigaglia, where the fair was held, her carriage was recognised by some of the people assembled, who instantly began to applaud her. At first they surrounded the vehicle, merely anxious to catch a glimpse of her, till some more hardy than the rest began to call on her to sing. This she refused to do, and begged of them to let her depart quietly: they, however, unharnessed the horses, and became authoritative in their demand. Finding they would not be pacified, or brought to any terms less than instant acquiescence, she called on De Beriot to accompany her, and taking out his violin, complied with their wishes.

It was a curious scene. The vociferous acclamations of the populace, at the conclusion of her song, so pleased Madame Malibran, that she often declared afterwards she never felt more proud than in the triumph she achieved over the stern feelings of this rude auditory. At Lucca she added new wreaths to her laurels by playing for the first time in an opera by Persiani, entitled "Ines de Castro." Her powerful talents rendered it highly successful.

All the young nobles of the Ducal court were sighing at the feet of Malibran. One evening

during her performance the Duke was taking
ices in his box, one of which he sent by a
courtier to the fair syren. But so jealous were
all the others, and so envious were they of him
who had been chosen to fulfil the mission, that
on his return the Duke broke the cup which
had contained the ice into twenty pieces, and
gave to each a fragment of the china which
had been blessed by the touch of the idol.

Her engagement with the Duke Visconti
called her back to Milan. There she was
received with rapture. Every night wreaths of
flowers, gold and silver bouquets, lines of
poetry, and purses—in fact, everything that
generosity and admiration could suggest, were
thrown to her on the stage. She was frequently
obliged to sing the same piece no less than
three times over. The Milanese looked upon
her as something superhuman.

Triumphs like these repay the artist for
those toils and annoyances which are only the
price at which such distinction can be earned.

After playing thirteen nights on very liberal

terms, Madame Malibran proceeded to Naples, where she had entered into an agreement to play forty nights at the rate of 2,000 francs for each performance, besides two free benefits.

She reappeared for the third time at Naples, on the 11th of November, at the Fondo Theatre. She selected the Somnambula for her *début*. The result proved that she could not have made a better choice. The audience were enraptured. Her peculiar mode of giving the passage,

" Io non son rea,"

in the first act, completely overpowered the feelings of all who heard her.

But who can describe the electrifying effect she produced in the finale?

" Ab ! non guinge uman pensiero
Al contento ond 'io sou piena."

By an ingenious transposition of the original phrase of Bellini, her voice descended to the tenor G; then by a rapid transition she struck the G above the treble stave, an interval of two octaves.

The phrase, as Bellini wrote it, is as follows.

- - vi-amo, ci for - miamo un ciel d'a-

mor, Ah nel-la ter - - - - - - ra in cui vi

via - - - - - - - mo, ci for - mia - - - - -

mo un ciel d'a - mor. etc.

Madame Malibran sang it thus:—

- - vi-amo, ci for-mia-mo un ciel d'a-

mor, Ah nel-la ter - - - - - - ra in cui vi-

via - - - - - - mo, ci, for-mia - - - mo un

ciel d'a - - mor etc.

I have here transcribed the notes; but none
can conceive the effect they produced, save those
who have heard them sung by Malibran. I
will not attempt to detail the numerous beauties
which she infused into this charming opera.
Suffice it to say, none ever did or ever will equal
her in it.

On the 19th she played in Tancredi at San
Carlos. Her reception was indifferent. The
part was never a favourite with her. She often
declared that Tancredi was an insignificant
being, with whose feelings she had no sympathy.
On the 4th of December she appeared in
Norma, and was highly applauded.

In every place in which Madame Malibran
performed, she left behind her some memorial
of her charitable disposition. She either sought
out and relieved some case of private distress,
presented a donation to some public institution,
or gave a concert for the benefit of the poor.

There resided in Naples at this time a poor
French hairdresser, who vainly struggled to

obtain a scanty livelihood. Madame Malibran sent for him, and desired him to attend daily to dress her hair, for which she paid him most extravagantly. As soon as he was gone, she would undo all his curling and plaiting, and again go through the operation of having her hair dressed by another *coiffeur*. Some friends remarked that she gave herself a great deal of useless trouble, and suggested that as she only employed the poor hairdresser for charity, it would be better to give him the money for doing nothing.

" O no !" replied she, " he is poor but proud; he thinks he earns the money, and consequently feels no humiliation in taking it. To receive reward is gratifying; to accept charity is degrading. Besides, when he hears my headdress praised, he believes it to be his handywork, and feels proud of his talents. To confer such happiness is worth any sacrifice."

CHAPTER XXIX.

THE Marquis de Louvois had not failed, according to his promise, to visit Naples. He became
the most intimate friend of Madame Malibran,
who thoroughly appreciated his superior merits;
whilst he, delighted with her unaffected frankness and excellent feeling, cordially returned
her friendship, and did everything in his power
to secure it.

The Marchioness de Lagrange, and the Marchioness de la Ferté, two French ladies of rank, likewise offered her their friendship. This was highly gratifying to Madame Malibran, and it amply atoned for the slights she received from the pseudo-aristocracy of Naples. An idea of their exclusiveness may be deduced from the following anecdote which occurred during this period.

Madame de L—— gave a grand masquerade; and desirous to make it as attractive as possible, she wished to secure the presence of Madame Malibran. But as distinction of classes was strictly preserved in "La Bella Napoli," the lady thought it would be better to separate the cantatrice from the rest of the company, and rank her as a professional person. To give her an opportunity of displaying her talents, she erected a tent in the middle of the grounds, in which Maria was to preside as a gipsy, and occasionally to sing. This plan was, however,

frustrated; several of the leading families inti-
mated to the lady " that if they were to associate
with an actress they should feel degraded, and
consequently declined attending the party." So
poor Madame de L—— was forced to give up
the presence of her favourite; but, from a
praiseworthy feeling of delicacy, she cautiously
concealed from Madame Malibran the reasons
which had induced her to alter the arrangements
for her party.

The ingenuity of Madame Malibran was
put to the test in Naples. Having no female
servant with her, she was compelled to arrange
and lay out all her theatrical dresses. Notwithstanding this, she had plenty of time to devote to
amusement.

One day, when at Castellmare, she formed
a gypsy party. The company, who were
mounted on donkeys, climbed the verdant rocks,
and penetrated the delightful thickets which deck
this favoured spot. On approaching the do-

main of the Prince of Capua, they saw posted
up a notice forbidding any one, under the
severest penalty, to intrude on the sacred boun-
daries of the Villa Cassina. The merry party,
led by Madame Malibran, passed this notifi-
cation without observing it. They had already
trespassed on the forbidden ground, when a
band of armed sbirri pounced upon them, threatening them with all the terrors of the Prince's
displeasure. Entreaty was vain,—bribery was
equally unavailing,—threats were laughed at,—
and resistance put out of the question by
numerical superiority. In this terrific dilemma,
Maria bethought herself of an expedient likely
to extricate herself and her friends ; namely, to
try the power of that voice to whose enchanting
spell thousands had bowed. She instantly
began to sing one of her finest morceaux. The
sbirri appeared transfixed with amazement. In
another moment their caps were doffed, and
the party were respectfully allowed to depart.

Like the head of Cerberus, which bowed to the lyre of Orpheus, these men were moved by the power of Malibran's captivating talents, and owned a sway as yet unknown to their rough natures.

CHAPTER XXX.

Road from Naples to Vomero—The Carmelite convent—Madame Malibran singing the Tarantula—The funeral procession—Madame Malibran and the priest—Hospitality of the monks.

LEAVING Naples in the direction of the northeast, the traveller reaches the road to Vomero. The road itself is so bad that few would be induced to traverse it, were it not for the picturesque views it presents.

The smiling scenery of Vomero, of the Villa Belvidera, and further on, the famous fort of St. Eluce, by turns claim admiration. The distant lake of Agnano, the lovely environs of

K 5

Puzzoli, next present themselves: and further
on is seen the summit of a sharp rock, or rather
mountain, on which is situated a convent of
Carmelites. These holy men live removed, as
it were, from the world, though in the neighbourhood of the world's gayest city.

On the little height in front of the convent,
having on its right Vesuvius, and on its left the
old crater of Solfatara, commanding a view
of the lovely Bay of Naples, sat Malibran one
fine autumnal day, surrounded by a band of
light-hearted friends. At intervals they danced
the merry tarantella, or, accompanied by cas-
tanets, they sang the favourite chorus,

La, la, ra, la, la, ra, la, au.

After which Maria would chime in,

Giu la luna in mezzo al mara
Mamma mia, si salterà
L'ora è bella per danzare
Chi è in amor non manchera.

And again the chorus was repeated,

La, la, ra, la, la, ra, la, au.

During this scene a sudden sound was heard,
a sort of gloomy echo, which in an instant
chilled every breast.   Another instant, and the
enigma was solved.   A procession of monks
was seen to issue from the convent, chanting
the De Profundis; they were bearing a brother's
corpse to the grave.   In a moment all was
hushed; the superstitious Neapolitans in a
moment stayed their mirth, and shuddered at
what they considered to be a fearful omen.
Madame Malibran alone evinced no sign of
fear.   She walked towards the convent.   Over
the door were inscribed the words, " Scomunica
per le donne."   She read this notice, yet she
boldly rang the bell.   A monk habited in white
came out and inquired what she wanted.

" Reverend father," said she, " can I be
permitted to see the convent?"

" Impossible, signora ; you see, by the inter-
diction inscribed over our gate, that females are
forbidden to enter.   Be kind enough, therefore,
to withdraw.   Ere you do so, however, let
me prove to you we are not inhospitable."

In a few minutes more a repast of fruit was sent out to Madame Malibran and her party. When they had partaken of it, and seemed to wish for no more, the priest again appeared. " Begone now," said he, " begone, and pray for us."

CHAPTER XXXI.

The new opera of Amelia—Madame Malibran dancing the
mazurka—Her love of dancing—Her deficiency in that accomplishment—Inez de Castro—Killing pigs in the streets
of Naples—Madame Malibran meets with an accident—
Her faith in the homœopathic system—Her performance of
Inez de Castro on the night after her accident—Her remark
to Mr. Young, the actor—A curious reply.

WHEN the King of Naples was not present at
the Opera, the audience warmly applauded
Madame Malibran, and thus repaid her for the
cold silence with which in the presence of royalty
they received her. She now began to display
her comic humour in several buffa parts, and
she played them beyond all praise.

On the 4th December she played in a new opera, entitled Amelia, composed by Rossi. The music was really very tolerable, and the piece by no means wanting in interest, but nevertheless it failed. In this opera Madame Malibran, by an extraordinary whim, undertook to dance the mazurka. She never excelled in dancing, although she was excessively fond of it. Her native grace seemed to forsake her whenever she attempted to dance. Still she seized every possible opportunity of dancing on the stage. In this instance Madame Malibran's mazurka certainly contributed to the failure of Amelia.

In Ines de Castro, on the 28th of January, she regained her laurels, and obliterated the failure of the preceding month. In the character of Persiani's heroine, she was so touching, so deeply tragic in the death scene, that several females were carried out of the theatre fainting.

Her success on this occasion was equalled only by that which she had achieved in Bologna. She was well supported by Duprez.

She was already announced to appear on the following evening in a new opera by Paccini, entitled the Colonello, with every prospect of success, when a sudden accident prevented her.

On the last Sunday of the carnival, during the festival of the *confetti*, she was driving along the Strado Toledo, on her way to dine with the Marchioness Lagrange. Her coachman was endeavouring to pass a narrow and crowded point at the end of the Villa Reale, when a pig escaped from the hands of a man who was about to kill him.* The animal rushed between the legs of Madame Malibran's horses, which instantly took fright, and set off at full

* In Naples they frequently kill pigs in the public streets, where these animals are allowed to go at large. They roam about until such time as their owners may think proper to kill them. They then go out and perform the work of slaughter, wherever they may chance to find the animal. A fire is lighted on the spot, and the carcass is prepared for the retail vender.

speed. They ran for a considerable distance ere they could be stopped in their progress. In the mean time poor Maria was flung from the carriage, (an open caleche,) and had her wrist dislocated. By good fortune a medical professor (Dr. H.) happened to be passing ; he had her instantly raised up and carried into the nearest house, where he set her wrist, and having bandaged it properly, had her conveyed to the residence of Madame de Lagrange.

The operation was very painful, but during her sufferings Madame Malibran thought only of the grief which the accident would cause to De Beriot. As Dr. H—— was quitting the room, she called him back. "Do not let Charles know how much I suffer," said she, "for I know how deeply it will grieve him."

The king next day sent his surgeon to Madame Malibran, but she refused to be bled according to his desire, declining any medical treatment, except that which was conformable with the homœopathic system, in which she had great faith. Her arm was much swollen, and she was advised to keep her bed. This, how-ever, she refused to do, and laughed at the idea. She had a case made to keep it in one position, and she played in Ines de Castro, the ˇnight after the accident, with such admirable address, that many refused to believe she could really have been so seriously injured.

Some short time after this, she said to Mr. Young, (the celebrated English tragedian,) " My dear friend, I have learned a good lesson by this. I find that hitherto I must have indulged in too much action in the part. I was compelled, in consequence of my accident, to be almost immovable, and yet I never received more applause. I'll act more quietly for the future."

One day an intimate friend accused her of being generally too tame in the opening scenes of her characters; her reply was curious. " I look upon the heads in the pit as one great mass of wax candles: if I were to light them up all at once, they would waste and soon burn out. But, by lighting gradually, I obtain in time a brilliant illumination. My system is to light up the public by degrees.

CHAPTER XXXII.

In the small circle of French persons of distinction assembled at Naples, Madame Malibran was received with open arms. Her gratitude for their kind reception of her was evinced by devoting her talents to their amusement whenever it was in her power. She would act parts in charades, (several of which were written for her by the Marquis de Louvois,) and was ever ready to sing when called on. In short, she

was the very soul of society wherever she
visited, enlivening by her brilliancy and wit
the dullest parties, diffusing mirth and good
humour wherever she appeared.

Madame Malibran at length bade adieu—alas!
an eternal adieu—to Naples.   She left that city
on Ash Wednesday, 1835.

On her departure she was followed to the
suburbs of the city by an immense concourse of
admirers, amongst whom some of the first
persons in Naples might be found, shouting out
their regrets at losing her, and their sincere
hopes that triumph and prosperity might attend
her.

Her carriage broke down at Arozzo.   Finding that it could not possibly be repaired in
less than two hours, she determined to take a
view of the town, and among other places she
visited the lunatic asylum.   She went straight
to it, accompanied by some friends who were
travelling with her.

The director of the establishment explained

to Madame Malibran the various cases of insanity, and the several modes of treatment; he stated that the general system was to humour and gratify every wish of the patients as far as possible.

"Do you think any of them would like to hear me sing?" inquired Madame Malibran.

"We have here," replied the director, " a young man whose madness is caused by having fallen in love with the queen. He is passionately fond of music, and I should certainly like to see the effect your singing would have on him. But I cannot venture to ask you to sing, since he begins to rave as soon as he sees a female."

"O! as to that," replied she, " I shall pass for a little boy, (she was dressed in male attire.) Let me see him."

Her wish was complied with. She entered the apartment in which the young man was confined For a moment he gazed on her with evident curiosity. Madame Malibran approached a piano which stood in the chamber, and ran her fingers over the keys. In an instant the poor maniac was all attention. She sang the romance in Otello. " Is this divine ?" exclaimed the young man, and he appeared violently excited. " No," he added, " this is the voice of a woman :" then bursting into tears, he threw himself into a chair and sobbed aloud. The director led Madame Malibran away, expressing his thanks for her kindness, and his firm conviction of the salutary effect it had produced on the mind of the unfortunate young man.

Several of the lunatics wished in their turn to sing to Madame Malibran, who very patiently listened to them, although the discordance of their tones was indescribably disagreeable.

Somewhat depressed in spirits by this visit, she left the establishment, after presenting a handsome donation for the patients. She continued her route by the way of Rome to Venice, where she had made an engagement to play six times for fifteen hundred francs (£600.)

Her reception was brilliant; but it is perhaps better to let her describe it in her own original manner. The following is a letter which she addressed to a friend on this occasion:

" 28th March, 1835.

" DEAR P——

" Don't scold me—do not believe me capable of forgetting you. The truth is, the emperor (whom may God have in his holy keeping!) has quite upset us, holding us all in hot water until he should decide on permitting us to appear on the 24th. As soon as this was fixed, we started for Venice. To describe to you the highly raised hopes of the Venetians would be too long; suffice it to say, my fame had reached them long ere I arrived, and they were all on the tiptoe of expectation.

" I must relate to you an incident that occurred previous to our arrival.

" You are aware that they have a lottery in
this city, and that, as in Naples, the lower
orders are very fond of trying their luck in it.
Like true Italians, full of every kind of superstition, my coming appeared to them a happy
omen; they therefore combined the four numbers connected with my appearance. Ten, the
cantatrice; * seventeen, the day of the month
on which I was first announced; twenty-four,
the date of my *début;* and six, the number of
my performances. Would you believe it? the
four numbers turned up prizes, and the very
lowest gainer won nine hundred Austrian livres.

" From this circumstance my arrival was
regarded as a happy augury to the city of
Venice, and I am followed about and cheered
by the people accordingly. My picture is in
every shop window, with lithographic sketches

* There being ten letters in that word.

of my accident at Naples. Thank Heaven, the pigs don't run about the streets here.

" I have made a great sensation in Venice by the taste with which I have fitted up my gondola; it is painted gray on the outside, red inside, with gold ornaments; it has blue curtains with rich tassels. My rowers are dressed in scarlet jackets, with black velvet collars, and cuffs, straw hats, with black ribbons twisted round them, and blue cloth trowsers. From this you may guess that wherever I go I am instantly recognised by my gondola.

" The fact is, I should fancy myself buried alive, if I ventured to enter one of those hearse-like black gondolas; I could not bring myself to do so. I was unable to appear on the 24th, as first proposed, in consequence of its falling on a very strict festival day. I therefore made my *début* in Otello on the 26th. To describe to you the enthusiasm with which I was received would be impossible."

VOL. I.   L

CHAPTER XXXIII.

MADAME MALIBRAN, as I have already stated,
possessed a singular talent for caricaturing;
but she never exercised this talent in a way to
wound the feelings of others. Her sketches
were incomparably droll, but not ill-natured.
Her great amusement was to sketch the profiles
of her operatic colleagues during the time of
performance, and this generally when she was
waiting between the side-scenes to come on. She
frequently took caricature likenesses of all the

performers in the green-room, and showed them to the parties themselves, who, knowing that no malice was intended, would be heartily amused.

Her facility in musical composition was not less remarkable. During rehearsal, whilst the hammering of the stage carpenters, the voices of the performers, and the din of the orchestra, were resounding in her ears, I have seen her, with a sheet of music and a pencil, busily at work, noting down, without labour or study, airs worthy of a first-rate composer.

When the Marquis de Louvois arrived at Florence, he found Madame Malibran engaged at the rehearsal of Norma. After some conversation, he alluded to an air which she had promised to write for him, and jokingly reproached her for having forgotten it.

" I confess," replied she, " that I had forgotten it: but no matter; it is not too late to remedy my fault. I will trouble you, sir, for

a leaf of music paper," continued she, addressing
the leader of the orchestra, " and a pencil."

They were handed to her: in a quarter of an
hour, notwithstanding the noise and confusion
which surrounded her, she composed a very
pretty romance.

In Venice she was constantly followed by
a crowd. If she entered a shop, hundreds instantly surrounded it. If she took an airing in
her gondola, (which, as I have before remarked,
was easily distinguishable,) a little flotilla con-
voyed her as she glided along. The quays
were lined by persons anxious to see her. Her
landing was watched for, and her progress to
her abode was a sort of triumphal procession.

One evening, after playing in the Somnambula, Madame Malibran was tempted by the
fineness of the night to sit for some time enjoying the breeze in her balcony, which overlooked
the canal. She had been seated there for some
time, repeating, unheard as she supposed, some

passages of the songs she had just been singing
at the theatre, when a gondola suddenly stopped
beneath her balcony. The next moment a
clear, finely-toned male voice, taking up the air
she had just finished, repeated it, but accompanied with words calculated to hurt her feelings, and which conveyed censure upon her
private conduct.

Between each verse the mysterious and in-
sulting serenader made a solemn pause, and then
recommenced his strain.

It was now midnight; no one but the mysterious singer was near, and Maria felt a superstitious awe creeping over her. But, determined to overcome it, she mustered all her
courage, and instantly sang to the same air a
few extempore lines, pointing out the impropriety of thus assailing an unoffending female,
and begging him to accept a few pieces of
silver. She wrapped the money in a piece of
paper, and having set light to it, that it might
not be lost in the dark, she threw it down to

the gondolier.   He carefully picked it up, seized his oars, and in another instant was out of sight.

On the 6th of March the Tribunal de Premiere Instance in Paris pronounced the marriage of Maria Garcia with M. Malibran to be null and void.   The husband had rendered himself subject to the laws of France by taking out his rights of citizenship during his last visit to that country.*   This decision once more restored Maria to happiness.

* See Appendix.

CHAPTER XXXIV.

Embarrassments of Signor Gallo—Madame Malibran's performance for his benefit—Crowded theatre—The *divina
cantatrice* — Herculean labour—Drilling an orchestra — A
panic—The white doves—Illuminated gondolas—The cup
of wine.

MARIA, having finished her engagement at the
Fenice theatre, was preparing to quit Venice
with a light heart, when she learned that Signor
Gallo, the manager of the secondary theatre in
that city, was about to become a bankrupt.
He was a worthy man; but having met with an
unusual series of misfortunes, he was on the
eve of failing. The moment she heard of his

embarrassments, Madame Malibran determined
on exerting herself to save him. That same
evening it was publicly announced that " Madame Malibran would appear in the Somnambula, at the second theatre, for the benefit
of Signor Gallo."

Every place in the house that could be secured was instantly taken. The idea of once
again hearing the *divina cantatrice*, for so they
had surnamed her, made every one flock to the
long-deserted theatre; and lucky were they
considered who could obtain the chance of once
more hearing her.

At the rising of the curtain, the house was
crammed to suffocation. Hundreds were waiting outside, clamorously, but vainly, demand-
ing to be admitted; and many a gondola was
seen gliding unwillingly away, whose disap-
pointed occupants had been turned from the
door.

Meanwhile Madame Malibran's task was
almost a Herculean labour. The company, as

might be expected under such circumstances, was most inefficient, and the orchestra still worse than the singers. In vain had Madame Malibran solicited the band of the Fenice to come to her assistance, and second her exertions. They all declined, and the labour of drilling the bad orchestra devolved wholly on herself.

At length the important evening came, and for a few moments all went on well. But no sooner did the tenor singer, who represented Elvino, advance to take his part in the duo, *Son geloso del zefiro errante*, than he was seized with a sudden panic, and totally forgot his part. Murmurs and pleasantries resounded through the pit; but Madame Malibran, without being in the least disconcerted, said in a low tone of voice to her trembling companion, " Sois tranquille, je vais t'aider;" and taking up the tenor part, she blended it with her own, singing passages of each alternately, making of the whole a beautifully arranged air. The tenor

L 5

singer by this means had time to recover himself, and was enabled to take up his part at the
close of the duo.

The audience, charmed by this example of
talent and presence of mind, expressed their
admiration by a tumultuous burst of applause.

When Madame Malibran arrived at the last
air, the gentlemen in the pit mounted on the
benches and waved their handkerchiefs, whilst
the ladies threw wreaths and nosegays on the
stage. With eyes streaming with tears, she
advanced to the front of the stage to return
thanks. At that moment two beautiful white
doves flew from one of the upper boxes, and
fluttered several times round the head of the
prima donna.

Meanwhile the populace on the outside of
the theatre were waiting patiently with a flotilla
of illuminated gondolas to convey Madame
Malibran home in procession; but she was so
overcome with ·agitation and fatigue, that she
slipped away in a hired boat. A vast multi-

tude of people collected around her well-known
bark, anxiously expecting her appearance; but
as soon as her departure was discovered, they
hurried after her, their torches shooting along
the surface of the water like meteors. Many
of the gondolas overtook Madame Malibran's
boat; and. the consequence was, that when the
fair syren came to her place of landing, a joyous
crowd were already assembled there, who received her with the demonstrations of honour
due to a queen, and greeted her on her passage
from the quay to her place of residence.

She had no sooner entered her house than
a deputation of gondoliers requested leave to
address her. They were admitted. The spokes-
man of the group stepped forward, and presenting a gilt cup filled with wine, he begged
her to touch it with her lips, ere they carried it
out to their comrades who were assembled
beneath her windows. Madame Malibran instantly complied with this request, and stepping
into the balcony, she raised the cup of wine to

her lips. The light of the numerous torches fell full on the manly and sunburnt countenances of the gondoliers, and produced a most picturesque and striking effect.

The deputation had now returned to their brethren, bearing the cup, and each gondolier in his turn raised it to his lips, and drank the health of Maria Malibran.

CHAPTER XXXV.

MADAME MALIBRAN was by no means insensible
to these marks of admiration and regard ; but
though elated at her success, and flattered by
these triumphs, yet they never inspired her
with feelings of self-importance or pride. I
have frequently heard her say, when speaking
of herself, " The severe manner in which I was
brought up to a certain extent soured my

temper; and I should have continued petulant and ill-humoured, but for the kindness I have experienced from my friends. That kindness has soothed my feelings, and filled me with gratitude."

. After spending a few days in Brussels, she again visited London, where she had concluded an engagement with Bunn (the manager of Drury Lane) to perform thirty nights, between the 1st of May and the 30th of July. For these performances she was to receive £3,775. She played in the Somnambula, in Fidelio, and in the Devil's Bridge.

The English are not an enthusiastic nation, but Madame Malibran had no reason to complain of their coldness to her. They applauded her in the most flattering manner, and never failed to encore her in the last air of the second act of Fidelio.

Madame Malibran was still unmarried, and consequently ill at ease. The following letter from De Beriot to a friend will best describe her situation.

" I much fear the Lucca affair will not be settled without our being forced to visit that city. Our impressario has not yet been able to come to any settlement with the government; we shall, therefore, be unable to start for Italy for some weeks. We have some thoughts of accepting terms at Covent Garden for the month of July. This is the best musical season ever known in London. We have concerts almost daily. The theatres are making a great deal of money, particularly Drury Lane. When Maria appears in the Somnambula, the house is always crowded. She is quite well, notwithstanding the extraordinary fatigue she undergoes. The following is a fair average of her daily labour: at nine, an hour's practice with the piano; at ten, rehearsal at the theatre; concerts from one till four; opera from seven till ten at night, and concerts again till daybreak; then poor Maria, wearied with her toil, snatches a few hours' repose ere she renews her drudgery on the succeeding day.

" All this is against my wish, but what can I do? She is, as you know, indefatigable, and refuses nothing. During her absence I frequently refuse offers in her name. If I allowed her to follow her own bent, she would certainly kill herself by fatigue.

" Fortunately she has got through the most harassing portion of her engagement. She played last night Fidelio, for the first time in English, with the most complete success. They made her give the last scene twice. Grisi has also been very successful in the Puritani. She and Maria are great friends, and constantly sing duets together at private parties. Since the days of Sontag, nothing so perfect has been heard. They are to sing the duet in Semiramide at our concert on the 20th of June; and as it will be the first time they have been heard together in public, I shall take care to announce it in a bill three yards long, containing letters of at least a foot in height. I reckon on a crowded room. By letters from Paris I am informed that we must yet wait ten months longer ere we can be married ; that being the period prescribed by law for widows to remain single. This annoys us much ; but even if we should get over this obstacle, there is still another which presents itself ; we have neither of us a domicile in Paris, which it is necessary to have previously to our marriage. We must be united in France, and act strictly according to French law, the divorce having been pro-. nounced according to the French code," &c.

No sooner had Madame Malibran completed her engagement in London than she started once more for Italy, having entered into terms with Azzolini to perform at Lucca. There however, she was destined to meet with disappointment. The cholera had just broken out in that part of Italy, the country was in a state of dire alarm, and not even the Opera was thought of.

Once or twice, it is true, the charms of the

fair warbler overcame the public fear. The theatre was frequented, and the inhabitants of Lucca once again listened with rapturous joy to their favourite. On one occasion a party of young men (many of whom were of the highest birth) unharnessed her horses, and dragged her in triumph to her residence, where they begged from her her bouquet, her gloves, her handkerchief, and her shawl, to be distributed as relics amongst them. On presenting herself at the window, she was greeted with loud cheers, whilst the military band of the garrison performed a new piece of music composed in honour of her arrival.

Madame Malibran left Lucca amid the regret of the inhabitants, who expressed sincere hopes that she might escape the ravages of the unsparing malady, which for a time stalked with demon strides through " sunny Italy."

CHAPTER XXXVI.

The cholera at Leghorn—Madame Malibran's letter to the Marquis de Louvois—Sanatory regulations—Journey to Milan—Dangers—Madame Malibran's courage—The muleteer.

THE day before Madame Malibran's departure from Lucca, the cholera broke out at Leghorn, where the quarantine laws were immediately put in force.

Before she quitted Lucca, Madame Malibran wrote the following letter to the Marquis de Louvois:

" 2nd September, 1835.

" .. . . . Come speedily to Milan. We are

off from this place as quick as we can go;
flying, not from the fear of the cholera, but the
prospect of the *cordons sanataires,* and a thousand other rigorous measures which this disorder
has introduced, to the utter destruction of my unfortunate impressario. *Non dico niente di noi.*
You must guess all about us. The Duke has
valiantly run away. The most pious D——
has done the same, and has forgotten to leave
any funds to meet the *choleric attack* to which
his retainers may be exposed. So be it. Some
folks take great care of themselves for the love
of God and their confessors, having before
them the wholesome proverb, *Qui trop embrasse
mal etreint.* . . . .

 " It appears that the Duke V——i is in a
dreadful panic about the cholera, and already
repents having engaged me. Nevertheless I
am told they expect me at Milan with *devotion,*
being fully persuaded my appearance will act as
a sort of camphor bag, and drive away infection.
As to me, I have no fear for myself; my only

horror is, playing to empty benches. I confess that is . . . .

"I believe there is but one remedy, and that is, to lead a gay life, to go to balls, eat and drink homœopathically, and leave the rest to Providence.

"I trust the marchioness is in good health. She was so kind to me, I can never be sufficiently grateful. I am out of spirits, for every body is speaking of cholera, death, and purgatory, till I fancy myself quite up to the neck in the latter. So I'll not annoy you further with my complaints, hoping soon to see you at Milan.

"Adieu—adieu. By-the-bye, pray write to good Monsieur ——, and tell him I've not forgotten him. I trust you received my first letter safe. I mentioned in it that we had spent a very pleasant day with Madame de Lagrange, who talked much of you. Adieu.

"I remain," &c.

The sanatory regulations adopted to check
the progress of the contagion were so severe,
that it was with difficulty Madame Malibran
could reach Milan, where she was bound to
appear in the beginning of September. That
month had now commenced, and she had only
a few hours left. The roads in the direction
of Modena were already guarded, for the dis-
ease had shown itself in that neighbourhood,
and no conveyances were allowed to pass.

Notwithstanding these obstacles, Madame
Malibran determined on fulfilling her engagement. One road only was open, but that
presented dangers and difficulties which no
female but herself would have dared to encounter. But Madame Malibran instantly resolved to travel by this latter road. Next
morning she started by way of Carrara and
Lavenza; but finding the quarantine laws extended there, she deemed it advisable to try
the mountain passage by Carrara, which was

nothing more than a mule-track formed along
the verge of several dreadful precipices.   Nothing daunted, Maria set out : a second carriage
followed her, containing some of her attendants.

To describe the difficulties, the imminent
dangers she encountered during this journey,
would be impossible.   In some parts the road
was so narrow, that while the wheels on one
side rested on terra firma, those on the other
were overhanging a terrible abyss, and were
supported by cords which it required about
thirty peasants to hold.

The hardy muleteers themselves often shrank
before the appalling terrors of the journey ; but
Madame Malibran encouraged them by her
cheerful smiles and her happy confidence.
With a look of gaiety and courage she accompanied them on horseback, occasionally singing
to them, and using every endeavour to keep up
their spirits.

As she passed through several miserable
villages, she bestowed charity on the wretched

inhabitants, who refused to believe she was anything less than a princess of the first rank.

At Carrara a poor sculptor requested that she would sit to him for her bust. She instantly alighted from her horse, gave him a sitting for half an hour, and then continued her journey.

Just before she arrived, a muleteer was thrown from his mule, which had suddenly become restive. Madame Malibran herself dressed his wounds, and when, on recovering, he declared his fear of again mounting, she instantly desired him to take her horse, and getting upon the mule, she soon brought the refractory animal to proper subjection.

CHAPTER XXXVII.

The cholera panic—Difficulty of obtaining food—Money received in basins of vinegar—Madame Malibran's engagement at Milan—Terms of her contract with Duke Visconti—Domzetti's Maria Stuardo—Political allusions—Suppression of the opera—High favour enjoyed by Madame Malibran at Milan—Attentions shown to her on her departure—Her arrival in Paris—Marriage of Madame Malibran and M. de Beriot—Musical party—Thalberg's performances on the piano-forte—Madame Malibran's donation to the poor.

NOTWITHSTANDING the courage with which Madame Malibran struggled against the difficulties of her journey, yet she had a still harder task in her endeavour to soothe the alarms of the panic-struck country people, who fled from the

approach of every stranger as from the har-
binger of death itself.

Our travellers were never allowed to stop
for a moment in a village or town. Permission
to enter was accompanied by a condition that
they should pass quickly through without halting.
They were frequently compelled to journey on
for four-and-twenty consecutive hours without
food, and were obliged to sleep in the open
air, or in some outhouse, where the rats, more
bold than the human species, failed not to visit
them during their slumbers.

When they got food, it was sometimes almost
thrown at them, and the money they paid for
it was received in basins of vinegar. The authorities read the bill of health exhibited to
them, at a distance. No person ventured to
come in contact with another. Never was
terror so generally prevalent.

In spite of these adverse circumstances, Madame Malibran arrived at Milan in good health
and spirits. Her reception was most flattering.

The following sketch of her agreement with Duke Visconti will show how highly her talents were appreciated.

" Four hundred and twenty thousand francs, (£16,800,) with a palace to lodge in, a carriage and a free table, for one hundred and eighty performances, to be distributed through five seasons, viz.

" Autumn 1835.

" Carnival commencing the 10th of December, and ending the 10th of March, 1836.

" Autumn 1836.

" Carnival, until March, 1837.

" Autumn 1837."

The two first seasons were the only ones which she was enabled to fulfil. She played in Otello, I Capuletti, La Somnambula, and in Vaccai's Giovanna Grey. She was also very successful in Domzetti's Maria Stuardo; but in consequence of several political allusions in that opera, it was after a few evenings withdrawn.

The energy with which Madame Malibran gave these points, created uneasiness in the government. This circumstance caused the suppression of that beautiful opera.

At Milan our fair *artiste* was courted by the very highest society. She was asked to every fete, and considered the chief ornament of every saloon.

On the day of her departure, every person of distinction in the place left their cards for her. At night, after her performance, she was conducted to her palace by a procession of young nobles bearing torches On her arrival at her residence, (the Palazzo Visconti,) she found the garden brilliantly illuminated, while a military band, stationed on the banks of the canal, played several grand airs. Next day, gold and silver medals were circulated among her admirers, exhibiting her likeness on the one side, and a complimentary allegory on the other.

She arrived in Paris about the end of March,

where every preparation was made for her marriage.

She now seemed to be restored to happiness, for the false position in which she had for so long been placed had always weighed heavily on her mind. She was anxious to become the wife of De Beriot, in order to calm the scruples of her conscience, and to possess a legal right to his affections. Every day she appeared to become more devotedly attached to him.

The marriage took place on the 20th of March, in presence of several of the mutual friends of the bride and bridegroom. The Marquis de Louvois and Monsieur Perignon were the official witnesses. In the evening they assembled at the residence of Monsieur Troupenas, the music publisher, where the party were entertained by a little concert. Madame de Beriot, her husband, Thalberg, and Rossini, were the principal performers. The joy which the occasion inspired, added a fresh charm to their superior talents. This was the first time

Madame Malibran had heard Thalberg, and she was quite enchanted by his performance.

That evening she gave one thousand francs to the poor of Paris.

CHAPTER XXXVIII.

The Gamin de Paris—Bouffé, the comic actor—Visit to Brussels—Concerts for the benefit of the Polish refugees—Return to London—Lord L.....—An equestrian party—Madame Malibran's horse takes fright—Her accident—She conceals it from De Beriot—Its serious consequences.

MADAME MALIBRAN remained only a few days in Paris, but, previously to her departure for Brussels, she visited several of the minor theatres. She saw Bouffé in the Gamin de Paris, and was delighted with his performance. She wept and laughed by turns, as he enacted the droll and the serious parts of this little piece.

On her return to Brussels she determined to remain quiet for some time at her residence at Ixelles, (half a league from the city,) but her active nature could not long endure this. She gave two concerts for the benefit of the Polish refugees, one at the concert rooms, and the other at the theatre. She was well received, and a large sum was collected. This was the last time she ever was heard in the Belgian capital, nor will the recollection of her seraphic tones be cherished less fervently than the benevolent feelings which prompted her to lend her talents in aid of the distressed and persecuted.

On the 19th of April she set out for London, where she was again received in the most flattering manner. Many even thought her voice improved, and I firmly believe such to have been the fact, for she never relinquished her practice and her endeavours to overcome certain weak notes in her voice. This was clearly perceptible to those who nightly heard her. Passages which she did not venture to try when she first visited England, she now executed with ease.

One day, during her stay in London, Lord L—— proposed an equestrian excursion, at the same time offering Madame Malibran the use of a fine horse, which he assured her was well trained to carry a lady. De Beriot was anxious to decline the offer. He was averse to it for several reasons; but as his wife was resolved to accept the invitation, any opposition on his part he knew would be fruitless. The party accordingly set off, but without him.

Madame Malibran, though a most courageous horsewoman, on this occasion showed evident signs of timidity. The instant the animal displayed the slightest symptom of spirit, she betrayed signs of alarm. This probably arose from the twofold circumstance of her recent want of practice in riding, and her being already advanced in pregnancy. The horse, finding her hand relax, began to increase his speed, and at length broke into a rapid gallop. Madame

Malibran saw a turnpike-gate before her, and beckoned to the keeper to shut it. The man, misunderstanding her gesture, threw the barrier wide open. The next moment the horse had got the bit between his teeth, and was dashing on at his utmost speed. Her companions, seeing her danger, instantly slackened their pace, thinking, if they approached her, that it would only tend to excite the horse, and increase the danger of the rider.

In a few seconds Madame Malibran felt the crutch which supported her knee give way, and the stirrup twist round her ankle.

A second turnpike was now in sight, but no one near to close it. The gate consisted merely of a bar, which lifted up and down, and having been left open, now overhung the road about twelve feet from the level of the ground. This was her only chance, and, like a drowning man grasping at a straw, she determined on springing upwards and catching at the bar, allowing her horse to leave her behind, in the hope that the bar would descend with her weight, and bring her safely to the ground. Throwing down the reins, she raised both her arms, and by a sudden spring caught a firm hold of the bar. But alas! her foot was entangled in the stirrup, and in another instant she was dragged along the ground by the now infuriated animal, her head dashing every moment against the flint stones which lay in the road. After being thus drawn for about thirty yards, her stirrup leather fortunately broke and released her. When her friends came up, they found her covered with blood. She had received several wounds in her head, and her face was frightfully cut. She was in a state of insensibility.

When she recovered, she found herself in bed in her own house. Her first question was, " Is my husband at home?" Being answered in the negative, she instantly rose, went to the looking-glass, and began washing the blood from her face and head, arranging her hair, so as to conceal as far as possible the accident which

had happened. M. Benedict, one of her intimate friends, at that moment called in. He
besought her to lie down again.

" Not for the world," said she, " It's a mere
trifle—I shall be better presently; all I desire
is, that it may be kept secret from De Beriot;
he will be miserable if he should hear of it."

" But seeing you in this state, he must
know it."

" He shall not know it, and I will perform
this evening as usual."

" Are you mad ?"

" Perhaps so; but I'll do it."

And again she endeavoured to hide, by every
means in her power, the wounds she had received.

When De Beriot returned in the evening, she
told him she had fallen down stairs, and thus
accounted for her appearance, having in the
interim written to Lord L——, begging of him
not to let De Beriot know how the accident had
really occurred.

That evening she sang at the theatre as

usual, but the seeds of death were already implanted in her. She neglected being bled, and she consulted no medical man. In a very short time she began to feel seriously the consequences of her imprudence.

CHAPTER XXXIX.

A lively letter—Concert at Liege—Father L....—M. Guis—
M. Mayerbeer—His hospitality at Naples—Monsieur and
Madame C——n—The Duke of Devonshire—Madame Mali-
bran's performance at Aix-la-Chapelle—Her château near
Paris.

ABOUT the end of July, Madame Malibran returned to Belgium, where, notwithstanding her
debilitated health, she gave a concert on the
12th of August.

By the following letter it will be seen how
lightly she could joke in a moment of severe
bodily suffering.

Brussels, 18th August, 1836.

"Of all the wicked, deceitful men on earth, you are the worst. You set my mouth watering by false promises, and then . . . . . . But, *n'importe*, I will never call you dear Father L—— again. I will scold you, although it goes against my heart to do so, if you do not start for Brussels the instant you receive this epistle.

"We shall remain here till the 14th, when there is a concert at Liege, where De Beriot will play, and I *squall*.

"It is now the 25th;* you can therefore spend a full fortnight with us. This is the least Father L—— can do to please his adopted children, without prejudice to little Jules. Your love for him should now be on the decrease, for he is of course getting older, and consequently more mischievous, more wicked, and more *wise*.

---

* This part of the letter would appear to have been written a week subsequently to the commencement.

" Tell him I don't forget him, and that I hope he is becoming generous and fond of truth, and that he keeps his hands and nails always clean. Do you recollect our fun at Venice? I wonder what has become of my friend *Vranzoni*, and our companion M——. Have you seen M. Guis? He left London in despair at not having met you, and desired me to remember him to you most kindly. So now I have executed his commission, though I had hoped to do so in person. Is M. Mayerbeer in France? Pray tell him I shall never forget his kind hospitality at Naples.

" I met the other day M. and Madame C———n in London; they affected scarcely to know me, fearful that any intimacy with me might injure them in public opinion, and more especially in that of their patron, the Duke of Devonshire. They cautiously shrank from every allusion to the many pleasant evenings we passed together at Naples. C ——n and his wife are people of the world, and only recognise those whose acquaintance can do them good. I confess I was foolish enough to feel vexed with these people, whose conduct is the more absurd, inasmuch as they were always glad to receive me at their own house, and come to mine, before the authorities were pleased to pronounce their formidable consent on that happy day, when your presence added much joy to the occasion.

" I have not heard one word lately about good Mamma L——. I wish you would tell me all about her and Minfili when you next write.

" Charles has very bad eyes, or he would himself indite a P. S. He desires me, however, to add his prayers to mine, and beseeches you to come soon to us.

" Adieu, dear father. I embrace you with all my heart."

A few weeks after this date, Madame Malibran played in the Somnambula at Aix-la-Chapelle, and then proceeded to France, where

she had purchased a small property (Le Château
de Roissy) near Paris.   There for a time, surrounded by her friends, she forgot her sufferings,
and became gayer than ever.

CHAPTER XL.

Madame Malibran's impaired health—Ballads of her composition—The Romance of Death—Benelli—Curious coincidence—Exuberant joy—Presentiment of early death—Madame Malibran's love of childish amusements—The Girolamo Theatre at Milan—Madame Malibran's peculiar tastes ascribable to her Moorish origin.

SINCE her accident, Madame Malibran had suffered from continual headaches and nervous attacks ; and though she never complained, yet her altered looks often betrayed her inward agony. In spite of indisposition, she continued to work hard at a set of ballads she had promised to compose. She would often labour at them with one hand, whilst with the other she pressed her throbbing temples, and endeavoured to allay the torture she suffered. Her anxiety to accomplish this task appeared like a presentiment that little of life was left her to finish it.

During her abode at Roissy, she composed the romance entitled Death ; the words were given her by Lablache, and were written by Benelli in a moment of sardonic gaiety.   They are as follows:

> Ton ton, chi batte là ?
> Ton ton, sono la morte,
> Ci cameriere bei presto,
> O là, apri le porte,
> Sono tré mesi.
> Che la salute in voce
> Essa mi prende à ginoco,
> Si mostra è se ne và,
> Io la salute in voce hà
> Essa mi prende à ginoco
> Si mostra, è se ne và ;
> Ecco villane vende mia

Conta co frà tim coro
Ebra si sta con loro.
Di mè, non hà pietà......
Ton ton, chi batte là ?
Ton ton, sono la morte.

It is curious that Benelli died two months after he wrote the above lines, and Madame Malibran died one month after she set them to music. This romance was her last composition.

Madame Malibran's alarming state of health did not prevent her from fully enjoying her happiness, in being at length the wife of the man she loved.

In the intervals between her severe fits of headache, I have seen her indulge in the most extravagant flow of spirits. She would run about, dance, disguise herself, paint her face to perform burlesque scenes: never was joy so exuberant.

One of the most remarkable traits in Madame Malibran's character was her presentiment of early death, which was unhappily but truly accomplished. She felt a firm conviction that she was to die in the flower of her age: that long ere even her girlish gaiety should have passed away, the grave was to receive her. This belief may in some degree account for many of her otherwise strange whims. Her desire, for instance, to indulge in the amusements of her childhood, appears to have arisen from this cause. She wished to preserve all her early pleasures, confident that when they ceased to gratify her, she was destined to die. She also loved toys to the last hour of her existence. She frequently nursed dolls with delight, and was in raptures when she went to the Girolamo Theatre (a puppet show) at Milan, which she frequently visited.

These seemingly puerile tastes may also perhaps be ascribed to her Moorish descent, which none could doubt, since it was legibly written in all her features, and shone conspicuously when anger or enthusiasm lighted up her speaking countenance. Her passion for dancing (in

which she never excelled) was also evidently
of African origin. Her tastes were certainly not
those of a European.

CHAPTER XLI.

Manners and habits of Madame Malibran—False and exagge-
·rated accounts—Her love of violent exercises—Madame
Malibran accused of the too free use of strong drinks—The
charge refuted—A nauseous beverage—Madame Malibran's
strict propriety of manners—Her uncontrollable vivacity—
Singular reply to De Beriot.

MANY false and exaggerated statements have
been made respecting Madame Malibran's manners and habits of life. To the charge of being
masculine she herself used to plead guilty, inasmuch as she was passionately fond of riding, and
indeed of all violent exercises. She delighted
in long walks. She would think nothing of
travelling day and night during the most incle-
ment weather; and sometimes taking the reins

herself, she would mount the coach-box, and drive amidst hail and snow. She was fond of skating, swimming, and fencing; in short, she excelled in every manly exercise. Yet who ever was more gentle in her domestic circle? Who could soothe the pillow of sickness with more delicate attention? Who, like Madame Malibran, could move the feelings by the truly feminine expression of grief ?

She has been accused of an over-indulgence in the use of strong drinks; but no allowance has been made for the fatigues she was forced to endure, and the consequent necessity of stimulus.

From this charge I can conscientiously exculpate her. Her favourite beverage was wine and water—she frequently took water only. When she had to sing, she was forced to take something to help her to sustain the exhaustion which necessarily attended her extraordinary exertions. On these occasions she usually had recourse to a mixture of coffee and white bur-

gundy, or rum, sweetened with a great quantity
of sugar.   She conceived that this strange com-
pound, diluted with hot water, imparted strength
to her voice.

One day Baron de Tremont happened to call
just as she was going to the theatre; she was
very much excited.

" What is the matter?" inquired the baron,
seeing her lips trembling with excitement, and
her eyes nearly starting out of her head—
" what is the matter?"

" I am half mad with rage," she replied.
" What do you think, baron? they say I am
addicted to drinking; but stay—you shall know
what I drink."

With these words she took a china cup from a
sideboard in the room, and, without giving the
poor baron time to resist, raised it to his lips,
and poured the contents into his mouth much
against his own will, for it proved to be a
nauseous mixture of honey, barley-water, and
extract of tar.

" That is not likely to intoxicate any one, I should think," added Maria, as she removed the cup from the lips of the baron; " and yet they say I indulge in strong drinks."

Her determination to overcome every obstacle which might prevent her from fulfilling her theatrical engagements, was another strong point in her character. To such an excess did she carry this determination, that she has been considered mad by several who were not well acquainted with her eccentric feelings.

On one occasion, after having dined at three o'clock, (as she usually did when she had to perform,) De Beriot was sitting at table with several friends, waiting till she was ready to proceed to the theatre, when, about six o'clock, she entered the room with an air of disappointment.

" What ails you, Maria?" inquired her husband.

" I have got a dreadful sore-throat," she

replied, " and am so hoarse I can't sing a
note."

" Never mind—think nothing of it. Be calm ;
agitation will only make it worse."

" No, I must try some remedy. Ah ! I see
something that will do me good ;" and before
De Beriot had time to arrest her arm, she had
seized the mustard-pot, and swallowed the
whole of its contents.

Of the charge of avarice I think those who
have read the foregoing pages will acquit her.
She was far from extravagant—she spent little
or nothing upon herself; but to relieve the distressed, or share her purse with the needy,
Maria Malibran was ever ready.

Her manners, though gay, were irreproach-
able. She delighted in what is called fun, yet she
never suffered the slightest liberty to be taken
with her. Those who knew her never ventured
even a " *double entendre*" in her presence.
She abhorred everything approaching to gross-

ness, and, in the midst of her g reatest hilarity, a single word verging on impropriety would recal her to the most serious mood.

Her *liaison* with De Beriot she looked upon as a marriage, though the law lingered ere it confirmed the fact by pronouncing a divorce from M. Malibran, whom she regarded merely as her nominal husband; and she frequently compared her first marriage to that of Esmeralda with the poet Gringoire in Notre Dame de Paris.

Her vivacity was almost superhuman. Frequently, on coming home from the theatre, she would begin dancing about, jumping over chairs, and playing all sorts of antics. When De Beriot endeavoured to dissuade her from these childish pranks, her answer was (like everything else she did) strange and original: " My dear Charles, you don't understand my nature. I cannot take premeditated repose; it can only come when I am compelled by exertion to have recourse to it. I cannot economise my strength

—I use it just as it comes.   When I try to restrain my flow of spirits, I feel as if I should be suffocated."

CHAPTER XLII.

Subterraneous vaults—Madame Malibran's inspection of them—Her pretended dream—She leaves Roissy to fulfil her engagements in England—Proceeds to Manchester—Her extraordinary state of excitement—Lablache—Rehearsal in the church—Effect of the organ on Madame Malibran—Hysterical fits—The duo in Andronico.

DURING her stay at Roissy, some workmen, whilst digging in her garden, discovered a range of vaults several feet below the surface of the earth. This naturally excited the curiosity of all the inmates of the château, and on the instant a party was formed to inspect the subterraneous vaults. Maria entreated most strenuously to be allowed to accompany them, but De Beriot firmly refused to allow her; the con-

sequence was, she was left at home, and on
the return of the company she was in an ill
humour, and retired early to rest.

At five o'clock next morning she rose, and
having put on a light robe de chambre, stole
out of the house unperceived by any one. She
went straight to the cottage of one of the
labourers who had discovered the caves, and
having got some persons to accompany her,
descended and examined the subterranean
chambers. This done, she returned privately
to the château, and appeared at the breakfast-
table as if nothing had happened. At dinner
she pretended she had had a strange dream,
during which she imagined herself in the vaults,
and proceeded to describe them so accurately
that every one was amazed. It was not until
many days after that she gave a clue to the
mystery.

Towards the end of September, Madame
Malibran quitted Roissy for England, where
she was anxiously looked for. She proceeded

almost immediately to Manchester, where she took up her abode in the same hotel as La-blache, for whom she felt a sincere friendship. Notwithstanding her alarming state of health, she determined to fulfil her engagements at the music-meetings and concerts, as she had agreed some time before.

On the evening of her arrival at Manchester, she was unusually gay; she played and sang for several hours, and wished Lablache to tell her which he liked best of her two last romances, " The Brigand," or " Death."

When she began the latter, her excitement was extraordinary. She became painfully agitated. Her powers so wonderfully developed themselves on this occasion, that Lablache became absolutely alarmed, and begged of De Beriot to make her retire to rest: this she did, after many entreaties.

Next day she attended rehearsal at the church, but no sooner did she hear the organ than she burst into tears: this was not looked upon as

anything strange, she being continually subject
to nervous attacks.   On the day following
she attended to take part in the oratorio about
to be performed in the church; but no sooner
did the notes of the organ again strike on her
ear than she burst into an uncontrollable fit of
laughter, and was carried out fainting.   She
soon recovered, when she came back and sang
with the greatest effect an air by Cimarosa.

In the evening she insisted on singing at the
theatre, and got through her task without apparent fatigue.   The following day she again
attempted to assist at the oratorio, but was
carried out of the church in a state of insensibility, which continued for several hours.   She
recovered in time to perform again at the
theatre, where, in spite of every opposition, she
insisted on going.   There, like a beautiful
spectre, she again presented herself.   Her personal appearance on this occasion bore the
impress of sickness; her countenance bespoke
suffering and melancholy, but never was her

voice finer or more powerful.   In the duet from
Andronico, which she sang with Madame Caradori, she was highly applauded.

The acclamations of thousands rang in her
ears, as, overcome by exertion, she tottered
from the orchestra; but when the cries of " *encore*" mingled with these cheers, her whole
strength appeared to return.   A new life seemed
to animate her; she drew herself up to her
full height, her eye suddenly kindled with
triumph, and once more returning, she grace-
fully acknowledged the compliment.   She sang
the duet a second time; but from the theatre
she was carried to her deathbed.

CHAPTER XLIII.

Alarming condition of Madame Malibran—Convulsion fits—
Proposal to bleed her—Alleged error in the mode of medical
treatment—Sensation excited by Madame Malibran's illness
—Her anxious inquiries requesting De Beriot's perform-
ance—Her last words—Dispute respecting her remains—
Chapel erected to her memory at Lacken.

SCARCELY had she reached her hotel, when she
was attacked by violent convulsions. A medical
gentleman was sent for, who, on his arrival,
wished to have her bled. Several of her friends
opposed this, but the doctor insisted on it; and
De Beriot being at that moment engaged in his
professional duties at the concert, there was
no one present who could interpose any autho-

rity as to the mode of treating the patient. Madame Malibran, who for a moment recovered her consciousness, said, " Let the doctor do as he wishes; it signifies but little now." She was accordingly bled. It has been alleged, though I believe erroneously, that this bleeding caused her death. It was certainly not judicious, but it could be of little consequence at that period. Had she been bled immediately after her fall from her horse, the probability is, that her life would have been preserved; but when the doctor was called in at Manchester, there appeared no ground for believing that any human skill could have preserved her.

The alarming illness of Madame Malibran caused the greatest sensation in Manchester. Every person of respectability called to inquire after her. The door of the hotel at which she resided was beset by an anxious crowd. The newspapers gave daily bulletins of the state of her health, and some hopes were for a time entertained of her ultimate recovery; but, alas!

her malady made awful strides. In two or three days all pain had left her, and she fell into a kind of stupor. For hours she lay without showing signs of life; or~e only did she again appear conscious of the passing scene, when, speaking with difficulty, she asked, " How De Beriot had played? whether he had been much applauded?" On being assured of his success, she smiled, sank back on her pillow, and never again spoke. Her soul fled without a sigh, without a struggle :—not a groan, not a start, accompanied her parting breath. For several minutes she had ceased to exist, ere those around her couch were aware of the fact.

The committee appointed for conducting the Manchester musical festival wished to pay De Beriot the full amount of his wife's engagement, though she had only performed twice. This he refused.

The disputes about the burial of her remains, and the anxiety of the people of Manchester to possess the sacred relic, prove how much they esteemed her. The subsequent exhumation, and other circumstances, are too well known to require further c mment.

A chapel s about to be erected over her tomb at Lacken, and her bust is to be placed in it. At that sacred shrine let her admirers devoutly kneel, and, while offering up a prayer, let them recal, as a beautiful dream, the tones of the once idolised Malibran !

END OF VOL I.

LONDON:
PRINTED BY IBOTSON AND PALMER,
SAVOY STREET.

CPSIA information can be obtained at www.ICGtesting.com
Printed in the USA
LVOW081747140912

298871LV00007B/46/A